SECRET SAVANNAH

A GUIDE TO THE WEIRD, WONDERFUL, AND OBSCURE

Christopher Berinato

Library of Congress Control Number: 2019936719

ISBN: 9781681062297

Design by Jill Halpin
Author photo by Shannon Zaller.

Printed in the United States of America
19 20 21 22 23 5 4 3 2 1

For my wife Courtney and my son Max who motivated me, inspired me, and explored Savannah with me.

CINEMATIC TREATS (page 118)

CONTENTS

INTRODUCTION

There is something wonderful about feeling like a tourist again in your own city. When you live in one place for an extended period of time, you begin to take for granted what it has to offer. I can't tell you how many times I've gotten blank looks from friends and locals when I ask them if they've heard of some of the unusual things to see in and around Savannah.

Have you seen the abandoned "castle" in the woods? Do you know what those palm trees on Victory Drive represent? Have you been in Alex Raskin's antique store? Have you done a napkin drawing at Abe's on Lincoln? Did you know the first photograph of a baseball game was taken at Fort Pulaski? Have you looked for old cartographic treasures at V&J Duncan's Antique Maps? Did you know that green house you drive by every day on Abercorn Street was built by a reality TV show? Have you hummed a tune at the Kazoo Museum? Have you stepped inside the smallest church in America? Have you visited the vivid papier-mâché sculptures in the lane behind Anderson Street? Do you even know who the Waving Girl is?

Secret Savannah is a sourcebook for visitors who want to approach the city of Savannah from a weird angle. It is also a refresher for locals who may have forgotten or ignored some of the quirks that have always been in plain sight. There are many hidden wonders and histories to discover in this book. *Secret Savannah* also covers some obvious touristy spots but peels back the layers to reveal why they may be more fascinating than you first assumed. For day-trippers, there are points of interest up and down the coasts of the Low Country and Coastal Empire, from Beaufort to Brunswick, and in nearby small towns with their own stories to tell. Hopefully, by the end of your journey, you will come away with a deeper appreciation of what makes the Hostess City one of the most charmingly strange places in the country.

THE SECRET GARDEN (page 20)

THE PALMS OF VICTORY DRIVE

What is the longest memorial in the country?

For motorists, Victory Drive has long been considered one of the most scenic roads in Savannah. Majestic oak trees loom over the traffic on either side with long wisps of Spanish moss dangling from their gnarled limbs. Blushing pink azalea bushes bloom in the spring brightening up the corridor, and orderly rows of palmetto trees (at its peak there were nearly 2,800) stand like soldiers in the median for miles.

Commercial development over the years has dulled Victory Drive's luster, so it is understandable that many people have forgotten that the stoic palm trees were meant to be a reminder of the men who gave their lives during World War I.

Victory Drive was originally a series of unpaved roads— Estill Avenue, King Street, and Dale Avenue—connecting the western limits of the city and Warsaw, a fishing village now known as the Town of Thunderbolt. When Dale Avenue was being extended and improved in 1919, city engineer William O' Driscoll Rockwell proposed naming the road Victory Avenue and planting an additional 135 sabal palmettos, with each tree representing a Chatham resident who died in the Great War. By 1922, the city

Victory Drive has a long history in Savannah—it was even used as a racetrack for America's first Grand Prix in 1908.

Left, *The memorial was moved from the median of Victory Drive to Daffin Park to make it easier to visit.* Right, *Although commercial development has sapped much of Victory Drive's beauty, there are still some areas along the stretch that still draw attention.*

named it Victory Drive and dedicated it as a World War I memorial.

In 1929, American Legion Post 36 and the Women's Federation of Savannah added a 14,200-pound granite monument with the names of the 135 soldiers, which sits at the corner of Daffin Park at the corner of Victory Drive and Waters Avenue. These days, the road has been extended even farther and runs 19.2 miles from Ogeechee Road to Tybee Island, so if you are planning on heading out to the beach, be sure to take a ride on the "longest palm-lined drive in America."

2 THE UNCANNY ECHO OF ROUSAKIS PLAZA

Did you hear that?

Many visitors come to Savannah for its reputation as a haven of supernatural activity. Chances of actually encountering a ghost here are pretty slim, but there is one example of unexplainable phenomena that is real and guaranteed to spook.

In Rousakis Plaza on Savannah's Riverwalk is a strange spot known as Echo Square. The small, bricked area is enclosed by squat planters full of pampas grass. Black pavers form a circle with an "X" in the middle. Anyone who stands in the center experiences a bizarre acoustic anomaly where their voice echoes back to them in disorienting surround sound. Most first-timers react with a mixture of shock and giddiness.

The strangest part is that nobody standing outside the circle can hear the echo. Many have tried to explain the anomaly, but there is still no official scientific word on what is causing it. It may be a combination of the sound bouncing between the buildings and the Savannah River and then focused by the planters. Sounds good, but then again, who really knows really?

The real question is whether the effect was intended by the designers of the square. It was never advertised as an echo chamber, and no plaque is set

ECHO SQUARE

WHAT: A little square with an anomalous echo

WHERE: East end of Rousakis Plaza, River Street, Savannah, GA

COST: Free

PRO TIP: If you're having trouble finding Echo Square, it's across from Bob's Your Uncle.

"X" marks the spot for Echo Square's baffling effect.

in the bricks to indicate that visitors are meant to stand in the middle of the "X" and laugh uncomfortably at the strange sound of their own voice reverberating around their head.

Adding to the mystery of Echo Square is that it remains relatively unknown despite resting in the middle of one of the busiest tourist spots in one of the nation's most historic cities. There is no queue of tourists waiting in line to try it out, and most people walk right past it, gazing at the river, blissfully unaware of its unusual characteristics. Anyone who does try it, however, is treated to one of the stranger activities the city has to offer.

Try not to look too crazy when you're talking and laughing to yourself.

3 THE COW THAT LOVED FLEAS

What is that giant cow doing on the side of the road?

Standing sentinel at the junction of GA 204 and HWY 17 is a "big cow" wearing a straw hat, gold jewelry, an "I love fleas" cowbell, and a permanently surprised expression. Kelly, who stands an imposing 15 ft. and weighs 1,500 lbs., is the mascot of Keller's Flea Market and has been drawing customers in since 2002.

Hubert Keller built his flea market in 1985 on an old mobile home lot and farming hay field. Over the years, the business has grown from a modest sixty stalls to more than 400 vendors and is now the largest flea market in the Southeast.

Wandering through the labyrinthine aisles, visitors will be amazed by the shear variety of unique goods—and junk—on display. It's a bit like Barter Town but without the "Thunderdome." Hungry customers can get some country cooking at Janie Arkwright's Kitchen, named after Hubert's favorite cook. There is even a barbershop for those who go to the flea market to get their hair done. The Kellers advertise it as a great place to have your garage sale, and, honestly, you would be hard-pressed to find another place where you can purchase a puppy, a used car, and a samurai sword all at the same convenient location.

In 2003, Keller's appeared on Turner South's Junkin' with Val and Dave.

Kelly the Cow's towering presence makes Keller's Flea Market hard to miss (or resist).

KELLY THE KELLER'S FLEA MARKET COW

WHAT: A 15-foot bovine beauty

WHERE: Keller's Flea Market, 5901, Ocheechee Road, Savannah, GA 31419

COST: Free (unless you find something to buy)

PRO TIP: Keller's is only open on the weekend, but you can see Kelly anytime.

Kelly the cow originally belonged to Roberd's Dairy until they shut down in the early 1980s. She spent the next two decades in front of Mammy's Kitchen on Ogeechee Road. Now that she stands in front of Keller's, with its folksy, trailer park charm, it is difficult to imagine her residing anywhere else.

4 THE WHOLE WORLD IN SAVANNAH

What is that giant globe?

If you are crossing the intersection of DeRenne Avenue and White Bluff Road, you cannot miss the giant globe looming over the surrounding buildings. The natural gas storage tank, which is sixty feet in diameter, was originally built in 1957 by the Savannah Gas Company and used for that purpose until the 1970s. Allegedly, Ted Turner's father, R.E. Turner, Jr., gave the company the idea to paint it to look like a globe. It was painted by Leo Berkemeier and another man to look like a school globe, and according to his grandson, Berkemeier fell from the structure during the job, sustaining serious injuries.

The original paint job showed all the national boundaries, but it was later painted to look like Earth as it appears from space. In 1998, international mural artist Eric Henn repainted the globe and included Hurricane Floyd threatening the Georgia coast, but it had to be fixed when it was pointed out that the hurricane was spinning the wrong way.

The globe has made appearances in a few movies, including *Forces of Nature* with Sandra Bullock and Ben

SAVANNAH GAS COMPANY GLOBE

WHAT: An impressive representation of our home planet

WHERE: 14 East 73rd Street, Savannah, GA 31405

COST: Free

PRO TIP: The globe sits on private property, but you can get pretty close without trespassing. Although it's not condoned, throwing rocks at the hollow metal globe produces a loud, satisfying laserlike ping.

Visitors who stray from the Historic District to the southside will be treated to one of Savannah's more unique landmarks.

Affleck, and *Dear Dictator* starring Michael Caine and Katie Holmes. If you think that the massive landmark would make a natural point of reference, you would be right. Many locals returning to town rely on the globe as an indicator that they are back in Savannah. In fact, until recently, there was a signpost next to the globe showing the distance in miles to various locations in the world, including Amsterdam, Tokyo, and Mumbai.

The globe even has its own lunar sidekick in the form of a moon-shaped mailbox on the property.

<u>5</u> TREAD LIGHTLY

Where are the Stone Stairs of Death?

Beware ye who traverse the infamous Stone Stairs of Death. The thirty-three steep, vertigo-inducing steps lead brave pedestrians from Bay Street down to River Street right next to Chuck's Bar. The stairs are so notorious for being dangerous that a yellow sign warns "HISTORIC STEPS: USE AT YOUR OWN RISK." A common pastime for locals is to watch drunk tourists shakily attempt to climb the stairs without tumbling down. Legs wobble, heels snap off shoes, and bodies slide down wet stones when it rains.

The death trap is the inspiration for the popular "Stone Stairs of Death" Facebook page, which is anonymously run by the most hilariously foulmouthed commentator in Savannah. The page is known for calling out and riling up local politicians for their scandalous behavior. The stairs are also the site of a charitable run called the Savannah Stone Stairs of Death Race—although considering how tricky the stairs are to run on, it could just be called

---

The Stone Stairs of Death blog has developed a cult following with "SSOD" bumper stickers adorning many cars.

The steps are not only steep, but cracked and worn from centuries of foot traffic.

"Death Race." In fact, the organizers acknowledge that running down the steps is tantamount to suicide, so the route only takes runners up the steps.

THE STONE STAIRS OF DEATH

WHAT: A vertigo-inducing set of stairs

WHERE: Next to Chuck's Bar, 301 West River Street, Savannah, GA 31401

COST: Free only if you don't incur medical bills

PRO TIP: Watch your step and try not to wear high heels.

<u>6</u> BOMB AT THE BEACH

What beast lurks in the shallows of Wassaw Sound?

If Godzilla is a metaphor for the atomic bomb, then Tybee Island has its own city-smashing monster slumbering off the coast, waiting perhaps to one day wake up and wreak destruction on Georgia shores. On February 5, 1958, an F-86 fighter jet had a midair collision with a B-47 bomber carrying a Mark 15 hydrogen bomb during a training exercise. The pilot of the F-86 managed to eject before his jet disintegrated, and the damaged bomber managed to make a harrowing emergency landing at Hunter Army Airfield but not before it jettisoned the 7,600-lb. bomb into the waters around Wassaw Sound so that it could lighten its load and prevent the bomb from exploding in the event they crashed. A ten-week search by 100 Navy personnel was unable to trace where the bomb fell.

There are conflicting reports as to just how catastrophically dangerous the bomb is, and initial claims by the government was that it contained a dummy trigger and didn't pose a threat unless it was disturbed. In 1994, however, a document was declassified that told a different story. According to 1966 Congressional testimony by then Assistant Secretary of Defense W.J. Howard to the U.S. Congressional Joint Committee on Atomic Energy, the lost weapon was a complete, fully functional bomb with a nuclear capsule. If that is the case and the bomb does indeed contain a plutonium trigger, the resulting explosion would include a fireball with a

One theory is that the bomb was recovered by a Soviet submarine, which is why it hasn't been located.

Beachgoers still enjoy Tybee Island, despite the looming threat hiding somewhere in the water. Inset, A Mark 15 nuclear bomb similar to the one lost in Georgia. (nuclearweaponarchive.org)

radius of more than a mile and thermal radiation up to ten times that distance. There are better ways to get a tan at Tybee Island.

In 2004, a private team led by retired Air Force Lt. Col. Derek Duke discovered high levels of radiation off the tip of Little Tybee that aligned with the description of where the bomb was possibly dropped, but a later investigation by the U.S. Air Force determined that the radiation came from natural deposits of monazite in the sand. In 2015, a satirical news site posted a phony story about a vacationing Canadian couple finding the bomb while scuba diving and it being finally retrieved. Alas, that is not true and it is (probably) still out there. Whether the bomb was stolen by the Russians or is buried under fifteen feet of silt, it is probably best to leave sleeping monsters lie.

TYBEE BOMB

WHAT: A lost nuclear bomb

WHERE: Somewhere in Wassaw Sound

COST: A trip to the beach is free, but a hunt for the bomb is probably costly.

PRO TIP: Little Tybee Island, a possible location of the bomb, is a nature preserve that can only be reached by boat. Blue River Marina offers boat rentals.

7 THE RUNWAY GRAVES

Who is buried under the Savannah/Hilton Head airport runway?

Gazing out the window of your plane as you close in for a landing at Savannah/Hilton Head airport, you may notice two oddly placed rectangles lying at a skewed angle in the runway. Most people assume that they are some sort of repair patch on the tarmac, but the truth is actually much more surprising. The parallel markers are the graves of Catherine and Richard Dotson, two of the original owners of the land where the airport is built.

Both of the Dotsons were born in 1779. The couple farmed the land—which at the time was known as Cherokee Hills—and were married for fifty years. Catherine passed away in 1877, and Richard followed seven years later. They were laid to rest next to each other in the family cemetery, which held about 100 graves, including those of slaves.

The couple rested peacefully there for decades until Uncle Sam came calling and needed the land for an airport. World War II was on the horizon, and the military needed a place to land its B-24 "Liberators" and B-17 "Flying Fortresses," that place being right on top of the cemetery. Almost all the graves were moved to Bonaventure Cemetery, but the Dotsons' descendants wouldn't consent to the matriarch and patriarch of the

DOTSON RUNWAY GRAVES

WHAT: The final resting place of Catherine and Richard Dotson

WHERE: Savannah/Hilton Head International Airport runway 10/28

COST: The price of your plane ticket

PRO TIP: Get a window seat.

Richard Dotson (1797–1884) and Catherine Dotson (1797–1877) get to remain on their land, even if planes land on them.

family being touched—they felt that it would have been Catherine and Richard's wish to remain in the soil they cultivated for most of their lives.

The airport may have paved over the Dotsons' graves, but they respectfully placed markers in their honor, and this being Savannah, you better believe pilots have a number of ghost stories to tell about the couple buried under the runway.

There are actually four graves, but John Dotson (1823–1857) and Daniel Hueston (1832–1857) rest next to the runway.

A CHURCH WITH HISTORY

Where was the "40 Acres and a Mule" order read to the public?

By the end of the eighteenth century, Savannah's First African Baptist Church—the oldest black church in America—had become so popular that the congregation had to split up to continue its rapid growth. In 1802, to accommodate the growing number of black churchgoers, the Second African Baptist Church was founded and built on the east side of the city on Greene Square. Run by Pastor Henry Cunningham—who was one of the city's richest antebellum black businessmen—the Second African Baptist Church quickly became the go-to church for the wealthier members of the free African-American community. The Second African Baptist Church is an important part of black history on its own merits, but there are some important historic events that took place there that really make it an important landmark.

When General William T. Sherman ended his March to the Sea in Savannah in 1865, he met with local African-American leaders to discuss what former slaves wanted to do with their new freedom. Based on their desire to live on their own land away from white society and former slave owners, Sherman drafted Special Field Order 15, which is commonly known as the "40 Acres and a Mule" order. On February 3, 1865, a few weeks after Sherman issued the order, Union officer Rufus Saxton

---

The original wooden church burned down, but a new building was built in 1925 and contains the original pulpit, prayer benches, and choir chairs.

Although the First African Baptist Church draws more visitors, the Second African Baptist Church has its own rich and unique history.

SECOND AFRICAN BAPTIST CHURCH

WHAT: An African-American church with significant history

WHERE: 123 Houston Street, Savannah, GA 31401

COST: Free but donations accepted

PRO TIP: The church is open to the public, and worship service is Sunday at 11:00 a.m.

read the order to a gathering of African-Americans in front of the Second African Baptist Church. Four hundred thousand acres of confiscated land in the region was to be doled out to the free people to farm and live (a mule was never actually part of the deal). Unfortunately, just a few months later, the order was revoked, the land was restored to its former white slave-holding owners, and 40,000 black families were left without a home, forcing them to become rent-paying sharecroppers.

A more positive historical moment occurred at this location 100 years later in 1963 when Dr. Martin Luther King, Jr., gave a version of his "I Have a Dream" speech to the congregation of the Second African Baptist Church before he gave his famous address on the steps of the Lincoln Memorial in Washington, D.C. Savannahians heard it here first.

9 TRESTLE OF TRAGEDY

What caused the Meldrim train explosion?

It was another typically hot and beautiful day in rural Meldrim, Georgia, on June 28, 1959. Nearly 175 revelers gathered on a sandbar under a train trestle on the Ogeechee River to swim, bask in the sun, and enjoy a relaxing Sunday afternoon with their families. What should have been a pleasant summer outing quickly became a nightmare that Georgians will never forget.

Seaboard Air Line freight train no. 82 was crossing the trestle dozens of feet above the swimmers' heads when something seemed amiss. Pieces of the wooden trestle began to fall into the water, and moments later a large section gave way, allowing sixteen rail cars to fall through to the ground. The natural response of the curious families was to move closer to inspect the damage, not realizing that two of the cars contained highly volatile propane gas. One of the cars was ruptured and leaking gas, forming what one witness described as "a fog." A spark, either from the train or a nearby barbecue, ignited the propane, creating a hellish ball of flame. The second gas car caught fire and exploded like a bomb instantly

---

A monument dedicated to those who died in the accident can be found in Meldrim Memorial Park.

No roads lead to the trestle and it can be reached only by river, making this memorial the only practical way to visit and honor the victims.

MELDRIM TRESTLE

WHAT: The site of a terrible disaster

WHERE: Meldrim Memorial Park, Canoochee Ave. S, Meldrim, GA 31302

COST: Free

PRO TIP: The railroad trestle runs over the Ogeechee River in Meldrim.

killing fourteen people and engulfing the area in an inferno that quickly rendered everything to ash.

The horrors of the scene are too terrible to describe, and twenty-three men, women, and children perished. After an investigation, it was determined that the accident was caused by the metal rails on the trestle shifting in the 100-degree weather, leading to the derailment of the cars.

THE SECRET GARDEN

Where can you visit a fragrant garden for the blind?

Savannah can be a feast for the olfactory senses, with the aroma of fine food wafting from restaurants and cafes or pungent jasmine blooming on the walls of historic homes (pay no mind to the sour stink of horse urine or the sulfuric tang of the paper mill and nearby marshes on certain days). One stop specifically designed to appeal to your nose is the Garden of Fragrance in Forsyth Park.

This secluded little spot sits innocuously in a whitewashed building hidden behind oak trees on the west side of the park. It is amazing how ignorable the garden can be—many people notice Forsyth Park's famous fountain, the outdoor stage, modern playground, and the grand expanse of lawn but can easily stroll past the garden without noticing it. Its three walls, remnants of one of the park's two military dummy forts, help to contain the scent of the flowers in the garden, while the front iron fence allows a view inside even when the garden is closed.

The garden was created by Jessie Dixon Sayler and the Trustee's Garden Club of Savannah with the help of landscape architect Georges Bignault. The garden was originally intended to serve the visually impaired and was called the Fragrant Garden for the Blind in Savannah. Its strongly scented flowers and pleasantly textured plants

FRAGRANT GARDEN

WHAT: A "secret" garden for the blind

WHERE: Forsyth Park, Savannah, GA

COST: Free

PRO TIP: Visit early because the gates lock at 2:00 p.m.

20

Although, the garden is not really a "secret", its position on the side of the park under the shade of trees makes it easy to disregard.

along with a gently bubbling fountain were meant to appeal to blind visitors so that they, too, could experience the splendors of Forsyth Park.

Over the years, the garden began to attract drug users and other criminal elements, leading to disrepair and the plants dying off. The garden was shut down and the gates permanently locked. Fortunately, the Trustees' Garden Club, Park and Tree Development, and the Junior League restored the building and replanted the garden, reopening it to the public in 2011.

The ornamental gates used to belong to Savannah's historic Union Station, which was torn down to make way for Interstate 16 just in time for the opening of the Fragrant Garden in 1963.

11 MUSEUM OR USED CAR LOT?

Where can you drive off in the exhibits of a museum?

Tony Vasquez had a problem. He sold vintage cars over the Internet and stored his treasured rides in a hot, muggy warehouse—not exactly the ideal place to show off his wares to prospective buyers. His solution was to open an inviting showroom that people from around the world could visit to see classic cars in a fun, family-friendly environment. As soon as word got out that Vasquez had a showroom, sellers flocked to him to help sell their cars on consignment in a space that is safer and better organized than the wild frontier of Craigslist.

Savannah Classic Cars and Museum opened its doors in 2018, and it is an ideal place to experience automotive history—or purchase a slick, classic Corvette. There are slot cars for children, video game–driving simulators to test your skills, oldies chiming from the stereo, a gift shop, and a mockup of a vintage gas station that whisks you back to the 1950s. Because Vasquez sells half a dozen vehicles a month, the inventory on exhibit is constantly rotating, making the museum ideal for repeat visits from die-hard car enthusiasts.

Savannah Classic Cars also does restoration work next door. Walking through the garage, visitors can witness unrecognizable hunks of rusted metal be transformed

Some of the cars displayed in the past include a purple 1931 Ford Model A Hot Rod, a 1977 Pontiac Can Am, and a 1954 Rolls Royce Silver Dawn.

Every classic vehicle is in pristine condition, and all the bright chrome and eye-popping colors will make car enthusiasts feel like a kid in a candy store.

into gleaming, mean machines. Another historical aspect of the museum is the space in which it was built. The old warehouse was originally built in 1954 and served as a box plant.

While most of the cars are for sale, Savannah Classic Cars occasionally displays special museum-quality vehicles. Who knows? Maybe they'll have the Batmobile on your next visit.

SAVANNAH CLASSIC CARS AND MUSEUM

WHAT: Museum and dealership for cool rides

WHERE: 249 E. Lathrop Avenue, Savannah, GA 31415

COST: $8.50 for adults, $4.25 for children 5–12

NOTEWORTHY: The building's original steel trusses were the last ever manufactured by Great Dane before they transitioned to building trailers.

THE OLD OAK TREE

What is the oldest known tree in Savannah?

Close your eyes and try to picture Savannah. What is the first image that comes mind? Is it the squares? The endless variety of historic architecture? The spooky cemeteries?

It's the trees, isn't it? The famed, Spanish moss-covered live oak trees really make a strong impression and visually set Savannah apart from almost any other city in the world. So, what is the most impressive tree in Savannah? The daddy tree? The one tree to rule them all?

Standing regally at the northwest corner of Forsyth park is the 300-year-old Candler Oak. The massive tree is 54 feet tall, with a circumference of 17 feet and a crown spread of 110 feet! If this old tree could talk (hopefully, it would be more like the wise Deku Tree from the *Legend of Zelda* series and less like those cantankerous apple trees from the *Wizard of Oz*), it would be able to tell us a lot about Savannah's history.

From 1819 to 1980, the land surrounding the tree belonged to hospitals—beginning with the Savannah House and Hospital and then Candler Hospital since 1930. During the Civil War, Union prisoners of war were held in stockades under the shade of the Candler Oak until General Sherman captured the city and the hospital.

Its limbs stretch out so far that
it requires wire suspension
to keep them aloft.

The Candler Oak Tree has endured a lot, but remains strong and healthy, even if it is held together with screws and cables.

Progress and the passage of time were not kind to the Candler Oak. It suffered a lot of damage from traffic and construction. By the early 1980s, the remaining life span of the tree was expected to be merely another twenty years. In 1982, the newly formed Savannah Tree Foundation made history by obtaining a conservation easement around the Candler Oak—the first for a single tree. The asphalt was removed from the ground over its roots, a fence was put up around it, 24-hour video surveillance was established, and a regular maintenance schedule was set up to ensure that the king of Savannah's live oaks would continue to live a long, healthy life.

CANDLER OAK TREE

WHAT: The oldest tree in Savannah

WHERE: 516 Drayton Street, Savannah, GA 34101

COST: Free

NOTEWORTHY: The property the tree stands on now belongs to the Savannah College of Art and Design.

13 SAVANNAH'S ST. BERNADETTE

Where can you visit a miniature version of a famed healing spring?

The shrine to the Lady of Lourdes in France is one of the most visited holy sites in the world. More than six million people visit Lourdes each year, many of whom are sick or disabled pilgrims, seeking healing from the spring's supposed miraculous powers. Thousands have claimed to have been healed by its waters, although the Catholic Church acknowledges only seventy of them to be actual miracles.

The shrine sits in a grotto that is the site where a 14-year-old girl named Bernadette Soubirous met an apparition of the Virgin Mary on February 11, 1858. Bernadette visited the grotto several more times with witnesses to meet Mary, none of whom saw the apparition, but did see Bernadette enter an alarming state of religious ecstasy. With each visit, the apparition revealed more information to Bernadette until the final meeting when it said, "Que soy Immaculada Concepcion (I am the Immaculate Conception)." After investigation, the Catholic Church confirmed that Bernadette's vision was real and built a church at the site. Bernadette was eventually canonized in 1933.

Many replicas of the revered shrine can be found around the nation and the world, but this one is certainly the closest. Just don't expect miracles from drinking the water.

A statue of St. Bernadette rapturously offers prayers to the Virgin Mary.

OUR LADY OF LOURDES GROTTO

WHAT: A replica of a holy shrine in France

WHERE: Our Lady of Lourdes Catholic Church, 501 S Coastal Hwy., Port Wentworth, GA 31407

COST: Free

PRO TIP: The church has daily masses if you would like to visit it as well.

What does this all have to do with Savannah? Well, you can save yourself an expensive trip to France because Our Lady of Lourdes Catholic Church in nearby Port Wentworth features a replica of the famed shrine and statue of the Blessed Virgin Mary. The small-scale version of the grotto was built by the church in 1958 as a symbol of multicultural faith in honor of the many Cajun people who came to work at the nearby sugar refinery.

14 SUGAR REFINERY EXPLOSION

Who does the statue of hands releasing doves honor?

On February 7, 2008, the Savannah area experienced one of its worst disasters in recent memory when a series of massive dust explosions at the Dixie Crystal sugar refinery killed fourteen people and injured forty. The refinery had been built on the banks of the Savannah River in 1916 and at the time was the primary source of employment for the residents of Port Wentworth.

Because the facilities were antiquated and not maintained well, there were many warning signs that the work environment was dangerous. Poor ventilation led to large amounts of sugar dust collecting in the rafters, on the floor, and in the basement. An overheated bearing on a conveyor belt ignited a blockage of sugar dust, causing an explosion that spread throughout the building, causing additional explosions. The powerful blast buckled the concrete floor, sending even more dust into the air, and witnesses from across the river could see pillars of fire several stories high erupt from the building.

Imperial Sugar modernized the plant by July 2009 and reopened the blast-damaged section the following November, much to the relief of employees hurting from the Recession.

The sculpture represents the hands of God releasing the souls of the victims to Heaven.

One year later, Imperial Sugar, owners of the refinery, erected a monument called Legacy Park in front of the building in honor of the victims and their families. The monument consists of fourteen black stones with the names of each victim etched in gold as well as eight benches. At the center is a beautiful sculpture of a pair of outreaching hands releasing fourteen doves into the air. The pain of the accident can still be felt today by families and friends of those lost, but this incredible monument shows they will never be forgotten. New regulations and actions will also hopefully ensure that such an accident never happens again.

SAVANNAH SUGAR REFINERY MEMORIAL

WHAT: A sculpture honoring those lost in a tragedy

WHERE: 201 Oxnard Drive, Port Wentworth, GA

COST: Free

NOTEWORTHY: In 1919, nearly 400 Cajun and Creole families came to Savannah from Louisiana to work at the sugar refinery.

15 LIGHTING THE WAY

How did ships safely reach Savannah?

If you are strolling though Emmet Park on Bay Street, you may notice what looks like a giant gaslight street lamp surrounded by anchors. Although it may resemble the other street lamps in town—just on a larger scale—it actually once served a completely different purpose.

During the Revolutionary War, the British scuttled many of their ships in the Savannah River channel to prevent American and French ships from getting through to Savannah Harbor. Seventy-five years later, the hulls of these six sunken vessels still posed a danger to ships entering the harbor. In 1855, J.F. Gilmer, Captain of Engineers, sent a request to the U.S. Lighthouse Board for a beacon to be erected in the city to help with navigation. A few years later, the Savannah Harbor Rear Range Light was placed on the east end of Bay Street as a companion to the lighthouse on Fig Island. With a cast-iron shaft, the lamp stands twenty-five feet tall with a focal plane of seventy-seven feet above the river.

THE OLD HARBOUR LIGHT

WHAT: A streetlight for the river

WHERE: Emmet Park on East Bay Street, Savannah, GA

COST: Free

NOTEWORTHY: During the Siege of Savannah by the French and Americans, the warship *Truite* shelled this area from her anchorage in Back River.

Changes in the channel's route rendered the harbor light obsolete, but the decommissioned lamp remained in place. In 1958, the Trustees Garden Club developed Emmet Park around what was by now commonly called the Old Harbor Light. By then, the light was deteriorating from salt water damage and had to be held erect with cables. In 2000, the Old Harbor Light was taken down and sent to a fabricator to clean off the rust and repaint it. It was relit a year later, and although it no longer serves its original function, the Old Harbor Light still metaphorically guides and welcomes people into Savannah.

Originally, the beam cast by the lamp was red, but it has since been replaced with a decorative gaslight.

THE MAN IN ELLIS SQUARE

Who is that laid-back statue reading a newspaper?

On a crowded day in Ellis Square, one could easily miss the memorial to one of Savannah's favorite sons. The life-size bronze statue of famed songwriter Johnny Mercer is so innocuous that it is pretty common to mistake it for an actual human being—well, on a dark day anyway. The statue, sculpted by local artist Susie Chisholm, is inspired by a photo of Mercer leaning against a fire hydrant reading a newspaper (featured on the cover of his collected works) and perfectly captures the lyrical genius who wrote some of the most beloved compositions in the American songbook.

Johnny Mercer was born in Savannah in 1909 and was returned home to be buried in Bonaventure Cemetery after his death in 1976. During his lifetime, Mercer wrote more than 1,500 songs and was nominated for nineteen Academy Awards, four of which he won. Mercer's most beloved song is "Moon River," written with Henry Mancini and made iconic by Audrey Hepburn in *Breakfast at Tiffany's*. Besides an Oscar, "Moon River" won the Grammy for Record of the Year and Song of the Year in 1962.

If the statue isn't enough for Mercer fans, they can visit his childhood home at 226 East Gwinnett Street or the Mercer-Williams House on Monterey Square, which

---

The bronze statue in Ellis Square was unveiled on Mercer's 100th birthday.

He may look like a casual everyman in this bronze depiction, but Johnny Mercer was one of America's greatest songwriters.

JOHNNY MERCER STATUE

WHAT: A tribute to one of the great American songwriters

WHERE: Ellis Square, Savannah, GA

COST: Free

PRO TIP: Try singing a Mercer tune while posing for a picture with the statue.

had been built for his great-grandfather General Hugh Weedon Mercer. The Mercer-Williams House was made famous in John Berendt's *Midnight in the Garden of Good and Evil* as the home where Jim Williams killed his lover, Danny Hansford.

KING-TISDELL COTTAGE

What is the only historic home in Savannah that was owned by African-Americans?

Savannah has many historic homes—the tourism industry depends on it—but only one of them belonged to an African-American family. The King-Tisdell Cottage is named after its former owners Sarah and Eugene King and Sarah's second husband, Robert Tisdell. Sarah and Eugene bought the house in 1925 and were prime examples of the entrepreneurial spirit that was thriving in the African-American community during the time—Sarah owned a confectionary business and Eugene owned a laundry.

The Victorian center hall cottage was built in 1896 by W.W. Aimar, and it is notable for its intricate gingerbread ornamentation on the porch and dormer in the wheel-and-spindle pattern. In 1980, the home was threatened by development until W.W. Law, a prominent civil rights leader and advocate for historic preservation, swept in and orchestrated having the house moved to a new location in the neighborhood of the Beach Institute.

The house is now used as a museum to preserve the city's African-American history and to showcase the culture and achievements of Savannah's

---

The house was moved from Ott Street to its present location on Huntingdon Street.

The house's beautiful gingerbread ornamentation and wheel patterns set it apart from other homes on the block.

African-American citizens. Exhibits in the King-Tisdell Cottage cover slavery and emancipation, black entrepreneurship in Savannah, Gullah-Geechee culture, and the life and achievements of founder W.W. Law.

KING-TISDELL COTTAGE

WHAT: The only African-American owned historical home in Savannah

WHERE: 514 E. Huntingdon Street, Savannah, GA

COST: $7 adults, $5 children

PRO TIP: You can experience the King-Tisdell Cottage by itself or as part of the Negro Heritage Trail Tour, which visits many other sites.

MOON RIVER GEECHEE

Where can you learn about Gullah culture?

A few miles south of downtown Savannah, on the banks of the Moon River—that's right, like the song—lies the small, isolated community of Pin Point. Founded in 1896 by freed slaves after the Civil War, Pin Point developed into a self-sustaining community of Gullah/Geechee people. Gullah culture developed in the low country of South Carolina and Georgia. Because of their isolation from white people, the Gullah people developed their own Creole language and a culture heavily influenced by West African traditions.

In 1926, A.S. Varn & Son Oyster Seafood Company set up a factory in Pin Point and became the main source of employment for the residents for several decades. While men gathered fish, oysters, fish, and crab, women cooked and shelled it all before it was canned and shipped all over the country. Craftspeople also built boats and made fishing nets. Unfortunately, by the 1950s ecological damage to the waters caused business to decline until the factory finally closed in 1985.

In recent years, the old factory has been converted into a museum dedicated to teaching visitors about

---

Although the community is small, it does boast one famous native. Supreme Court Justice Clarence Thomas was born in Pin Point in 1948.

Oyster shells pave the paths between buildings, directly connecting the site to its past connection to the river.

Gullah culture and the region's seafood industry. Through multimedia exhibits and demonstrations, visitors will learn about a marine lifestyle dependent on the coastal waters of Georgia and the enduring community of the Gullah/Geechee people. Pin Point remains one of the last remaining Gullah/Geechee cultures in the Sea Island region, so it is a vital part of preserving the South's African-American heritage and history.

19 BROADWAY ON BULL STREET

Did John Wilkes Booth perform in Savannah's historic theatre?

Are you looking to catch a show? Savannah has several beautiful historic theaters to choose from, but only one has the distinction of being the oldest continuously operating theater in the nation. The Savannah Theatre opened its doors in 1818 with a production of *The Soldier's Daughter* and is remarkably still running 200 years later. It was designed by famed architect William Jay, who also designed Savannah's Owens-Thomas House and the Telfair Museum. Thanks to hurricanes and fires, however, it has since experienced a few remodels in the two centuries it's been entertaining Savannah. The most recent renovation took place in 1948 when it was converted into a cinema and given the stylish art deco look that remains today.

Over the centuries, the Savannah Theatre has hosted some notable performers, including Oscar Wilde, E.H. Sothern, Lillian Russell, Fanny Davenport, Julia Marlowe, Otis Skinner, and W.C. Fields. There are some rather infamous moments in the theatre's history as well. Edwin Booth acted several times at the Savannah Theatre in Shakespearean productions, and although it has never been confirmed, it stands to reason that his

HISTORIC SAVANNAH THEATRE

WHAT: The oldest theater in America

WHERE: 222 Bull Street, Savannah, GA 31401

COST: $39 adults, $19 children

PRO TIP: Every show is a blast, so it doesn't matter which one you see.

The classic theater has a museum in the lobby that includes past actor photos and newspaper articles.

brother, John Wilkes Booth, also likely performed there at one time or another. A similar notorious figure from that period addressed an audience from that stage. On March 21, 1861—back when the theatre was known as the Athenaeum—Confederate Vice President Alexander H. Stephens gave his racist "Cornerstone Address" just a few weeks before the Civil War began. In his speech, Stephens defended slavery and white supremacy, laying out the Confederacy's justification for seceding—but don't hold that against the theater.

These days the company that runs the Savannah Theatre puts on regular Broadway-style live shows and concerts—including a beloved annual Christmas show—keeping the tradition of entertaining locals and tourists alive.

Baseball legend Ty Cobb even took to the Savannah Theatre stage for a role in *The College Widow* in 1911.

20 THELMA AND LOUISE

Why are there elephants in front of a fireworks store?

When special occasions come along that require a bang, Savannah locals hop across the river into South Carolina to purchase bigger, badder fireworks than what are offered legally in Georgia. Firework shops are a dime a dozen in South Carolina, which has some of the slackest fireworks laws in the country—almost anything goes short of hand grenades. One spot that stands out in the crowded explosives market is Papa Joe's Fireworks off of U.S. 17 in Hardeeville.

Even drivers not seeking mortars and bottle rockets feel compelled to pull into Papa Joe's parking lot because of a couple of impressive, eye-catching sentinels. The duo of Big Al and Lizzie are massive, life-sized fiberglass elephant statues that greet customers when they pull into Papa Joe's. One of them is a natural grey, and the other is—no, you're not drunk—bright pink! The popular pair of pachyderms—which are also sometimes referred to as Thelma and Louise by locals—are always a draw for passing families looking for a quick photoshoot, and they are kept in great condition with regular paint touch-ups.

Papa Joe himself bought the elephants in Alabama and had them shipped to South Carolina, knowing there

According to a former employee, the elephants used to wear sunglasses, but they were constantly breaking and were permanently removed.

Big Al and Lizzie always look fresh and nicely detailed, even if Papa Joe's sign has seen better days.

was something special about them. Big Al and Lizzie don't fit any particular theme or relate to the fireworks business in any way, but they do the trick in getting people to stop at Papa Joe's shop instead of the many other whacky fireworks emporiums that dot highways across the state.

BIG AL AND LIZZIE

WHAT: A pair of elephant sentries

WHERE: Papa Joe's Fireworks, 15794 Whyte Hardee Blvd., Hardeeville, SC

COST: Free unless you want some sparklers

NOTEWORTHY: If you don't care for elephants, their other location, Crazy Joe's, has a giant rocket in front of it.

ENDLESS RUNNER

Who is that lady always jogging at Lake Mayer?

Lake Mayer Community Park in the south side of Savannah is an oasis for residents looking for nature and outdoor recreation in the city. The sunny park offers tennis courts, a dirt RC car racetrack, a baseball diamond, playgrounds, basketball courts, a street hockey rink, and a rad skatepark. Sailing lessons are given on the lake, and families can always be found picnicking, fishing, and feeding geese along the edge of the water.

Even though there is so much to do at Lake Mayer, its biggest draw is the 1.43-mile soft running trail that circumnavigates the lake. Every morning the number of walking clubs and runners that populate the track—even on Savannah's notoriously hot days—have a symbol devoted to their efforts that keeps them motivated. A lifelike bronze statue of a smiling runner frozen in midstride stands at the entrance of Lake Mayer. The statue is of Julie Backus Smith, a former Chatham County commissioner and community activist who died in 2003. She was an avid runner who was the first woman from

Smith's burial plot in Bonaventure Cemetery also features a bronze statue of her jogging, although this one is now green with oxidation and rather spooky looking considering the surrounding atmosphere of old shadowy graves.

The life-like details of the statue even include a watch in its hand to keep pace.

JULIE BACKUS SMITH STATUE

WHAT: Lake Mayer Jogger

WHERE: Lake Mayer Community Park, 1850 E. Montgomery Crossroads, Savannah, GA

COST: Free

PRO TIP: If you go for a jog, watch out for angry swans and duck poop.

our city to compete in the Boston Marathon and at one point earned the title of fastest woman in Savannah. The sculpture was created by Susie Chisholm (the same artist who sculpted the Johnny Mercer statue in Ellis Square) and was commissioned by Smith's mother, who wanted something special to accompany the trail—which is also named after Smith—around Lake Mayer.

22

WHAT'S THE PASSWORD?

Where can you drink at a speakeasy and learn about Prohibition?

One of the nicest perks of being in Savannah is that you can walk around in broad daylight through the Historic District with an alcoholic beverage in hand (it's a boon for ghost tours, since how else are you going to see a supernatural apparition?). Savannah is a hard-drinking city, and if you don't believe it, come visit on St. Patrick's Day. Because drinking is so ingrained in the culture of Savannah, it makes brilliant sense that the only museum in the country dedicated to the Prohibition era would be located here.

The American Prohibition Museum, owned and operated by Historic Tours of America, provides an immersive journey through the history of the temperance movement, rumrunners, moonshiners, flappers, and gangsters. The two-story museum features thirteen interactive exhibits with history films, realistic sets, and eerily realistic wax figures by Potter's Wax Museum of St. Augustine. There is a figure of Billy Sunday, who famously called Savannah the wickedest city in the world. When you meet the frightening wax likeness of Carrie Nation, one of the most radical leaders of the temperance movement who made a name for herself hacking up bars with a hatchet like a Jesus-loving Jason Voorhees, you might decide to give up alcohol on the spot.

AMERICAN PROHIBITION MUSEUM

WHAT: A museum dedicated to America's gangster era

WHERE: 209 West St. Julien Street, Savannah GA

COST: $13.48 adults, $9.63 children

PRO TIP: For authenticity's sake, you're going to have to learn the password to get into the speakeasy.

The wonderfully expressive wax scenes really bring the Prohibition era to life.

But, if you don't, there is a treat waiting at the end of the museum's tour.

The museum has its very own authentic speakeasy on the top floor called 220 Congress Street Up. The speakeasy serves Prohibition-era cocktails to museum visitors during the day, but at night Thursday through Saturday, the bar has a separate street-level entrance for regular imbibers. As the museum advertises, it's "not your typical dry museum."

Speakeasies were once known as "Blind Pigs," and moonshine was called "white lightning."

23 THE GOOGLY EYE BANDITS

"Who did this?!"

Sometimes, bad publicity can be good publicity. In the case of Nathanael Greene, a patriot general who fought with George Washington during the Revolutionary War, not too many people besides historians and Georgians really knew who he was until a little prank brought him to national attention.

In October 2018, the City of Savannah Government posted on their Facebook page a photo of the statue of Nathanael Greene that stands in Johnson Square with a pair of googly eyes glued onto its face. The picture was, frankly, hilarious, but the response by city officials was so irate that it made the situation seem even funnier. The post read, "Who did this?! Someone placed googly eyes on our historic #NathanaelGreene statue in #JohnsonSquare. It may look funny but harming our historic monuments and public property is no laughing matter, in fact, it's a crime."

Locals got a good laugh from the prank, but the harsh reaction from the city caused the incident to quickly go viral, sparking Twitter jokes, copycat "googly eye bandits," and even T-shirts. As Trevor Noah said about the prank when he covered it on Comedy Central's *Daily Show*, "If

NATHANAEL GREENE MONUMENT

WHAT: The target of an infamous prank

WHERE: Johnson Square, Savannah, GA

COST: Free

NOTEWORTHY: Greene was originally buried in Colonial Park Cemetery, but his remains were moved to Johnson Square in 1902. It took quite awhile, however, to identify him from the other piles of dusty bones in the tomb.

Left, *Greene greatly contributed to winning the American Revolution, and along with Washington was one of only two Continental generals to serve throughout the entire American Revolution. Above, Greene looked just as surprised as city officials to find googly eyes glued to his face. (City of Savannah Government.)*

you want to find a murderer, yeah, put his mugshot on the news, but if you want to stop people from putting googly eyes on statues, don't show them how funny it is."

The city, of course, has since removed the googly eyes from Nathanael Greene's visage, but you can still visit the monument—which is also his final resting place—and learn more about his role in Georgia history. Really, though, please do not vandalize Savannah's monuments.

From afar, you could hardly notice the googly eyes, but from up close, Greene's stare was pretty intense.

24 PLANET OF THE GEEKS

Where can you get a dose of nerd nostalgia?

If eBay were a physical store, it might look a lot like Planet Fun. Located on Broughton Street—the primary shopping strip in downtown Savannah—Planet Fun functions as much as a museum and a retail space. Founded by SCAD animation graduate John Croley, the vintage toy and game shop is packed to the ceiling with plastic memories from your childhood.

Large glass cases display rows upon rows of classic action figures, such as G.I. Joe, Star Wars, He-Man, Transformers, Teenage Mutant Ninja Turtles, and Power Rangers. The collection represents five decades worth of posable heroes. For otaku, other cases have such Japanese toys as Dragonball, Gundam, and Kamen Rider. Boxes and shelves full of comic books and Japanese manga beckon to be read, and arcade machines in the back are hungry for quarters.

The biggest draw is Planet Fun's collection of thousands of video games from every console and era: Nintendo, Sega, Atari, Xbox, and all of the obscure ones in between. Sure, you can buy PlayStation 4 anywhere, but what brick-and-mortar stores have you stepped into lately that have a 1978 Magnavox Odyssey 2?

In 2014, Planet Fun moved a block over and quadrupled its size.

There is something for everyone at Planet Fun, but the owner says they could always use more "girl" toys.

In a city obsessed with historic preservation, Planet Fun is doing its part to preserve a piece of American culture. There are few places in the world short of Disney World that can elicit the same bright-eyed glee in children and parents alike. Whether you were born in the '70s, '80s, or later, chances are you will walk out of Planet Fun clutching your favorite plaything from when you were a child.

PLANET FUN

WHAT: A toy lover's paradise

WHERE: 127 East Broughton Street, Savannah, GA

COST: Free to look, but good luck leaving without buying something

PRO TIP: They also purchase old toys, so you may want to dig in your basement before you visit.

25 A FACE ON THE WALL

Whose face is on the side of the courthouse building?

The Tomochichi Federal Building and U.S. Courthouse is one of the more impressive works of architecture in Savannah. Built in 1899, with an expansion added in 1932, the massive building was designed in the Second Renaissance Revival style. It occupies an entire block and is constructed almost entirely of white Georgia marble.

The courthouse contains loads of features and ornamentation that make it a feast of architectural beauty, such as varied fenestration, a 150-foot bell tower, and richly detailed friezes depicting animals, fruit, and flowers. With so much to take in visually, it is easy to miss the two rather devilish, smirking faces on the north and south sides of the building. There isn't any concrete confirmation about who the sculptures depict, but it is commonly believed that they are supposed to be Jeremiah O'Rourke—he was the architect who designed the building, after all.

If the faces do belong to O'Rourke, then their appearance poses some questions. Did O'Rourke include the sculptures himself out of vanity, or were they added by someone else during construction? And why does the expression on the faces appear so sinister? Many tour

TOMOCHICHI FEDERAL BUILDING AND U.S. COURTHOUSE

WHAT: The strange relief of an architect

WHERE: 125-127 Bull Street, Wright Square, Savannah, GA

COST: Free

PRO TIP: The small sculptures—one on each side of the building—are located on the second floor between two windows.

Along with the U.S. District Court, the building also housed the U.S. Post Office until 1999.

guides and locals point out that the sculpture's pointy, goatlike beard paired with the arches emerging from his head like curved horns make the image of O'Rourke look intentionally pagan. Considering that O'Rourke is primarily known for designing Roman Catholic churches, it is curious why his appearance on the courthouse looks so Mephistophelian.

The site of the building is also notable, as it once held a courthouse that John Wesley, founder of Methodism, preached in from 1736 to 1737.

26 TREASURE ISLAND?

What was the hiding place for an infamous pirate?

In the early eighteenth century, Edward Teach, also known as Blackbeard the pirate, terrorized the coasts of Georgia and South Carolina, conducting raids on merchant ships and pillaging everywhere he went. Blackbeard's fearsome appearance, with his long, dark beard and burning matches stuck in his hat, earned him a legendary reputation—he is the prototypical pirate that all other pirates are based on.

Like any criminal, Blackbeard and his fleet needed places to lie low every once in a while. One such hideout was an island just north of Sapelo Island, where he would conduct his "banking." Georgia's creeks, marshes, and winding inlets made this island ideal for hiding himself . . . and his treasure. In 1760, the island was given the name Blackbeard Island by surveyors William DeBrahm and Henry Yonge and has retained that name ever since.

Over the next 200 years, Blackbeard Island served other purposes other than a pirate hideout. In 1800, it was sold to the U.S. Navy as a federal timber reserve since the trees in this area were ideal for shipbuilding. Then in 1880, a quarantine station was built there in response to the yellow fever epidemic of 1876. The quarantine station was shut down in 1909, and the only structure that survives today is, ominously, the crematory.

The island is now a refuge for loggerhead sea turtles and migratory birds during the winter.

Blackbeard was killed in a battle with Royal Navy Lieutenant Robert Maynard, who returned home with Blackbeard's head hanging from his sloop.

BLACKBEARD ISLAND NATIONAL WILDLIFE REFUGE

WHAT: The hideout of a dreaded pirate

WHERE: Blackbeard Island, GA

COST: The cost of a hunting permit or fishing license

PRO TIP: Blackbeard Island organizes a 3-day bow hunting trip for white-tailed deer and feral hogs.

Blackbeard Island was established as a national wildlife preserve in 1924, but legends of Blackbeard's buried treasure still persist. The last official treasure hunt took place in the 1880s, but nothing was ever found. Sure, it's possible that there is pirate treasure somewhere on the island, but don't bother looking for it, as artifact hunting is against federal law—so put down that shovel.

27 BUDDY COP CARS

Why are those cars parked in front of the police station?

Built in 1870, the old "barracks" on the corner of Habersham and Oglethorpe is still used as the headquarters of the Savannah Police Department. Back in 1895, the police department had a stable and relied on horses, horse-drawn wagons, and bicycles to get around. In 1921, they entered the modern era of policing by upgrading to eleven police cars. Since then, cars, with their flashing lights and screaming sirens, have been an important tool and symbol of law enforcement.

In 2003, after forty years of discussion and planning, the Savannah city and county police departments combined their resources and merged into one entity. To commemorate the merger, two classic police cars were permanently parked in front of the old Savannah Police barracks—a 1947 Chevrolet Bel-Air and a 1953 Chevrolet Stylemaster police car.

When the cars were vandalized by a drunken airman in 2010, their broken windows and taillights were quickly restored—although finding old parts was tricky. When they were returned to their spot in front of the barracks, then Police Chief Willie Lovett said, "It is extremely nice to have our vehicles back. While they were gone, it was like not being fully dressed. Those vehicles have become

Downtown police still ride horses, or "hayburners," when patrolling the streets and squares.

Top, *Although the police drive modern vehicles, it might be fun to be taken "downtown" in one of these classic rides.* Bottom, *Don't drink and drive.*

part of the old Savannah and Chatham police culture, and a very interesting tourist attraction."

By 2018, the merger turned out to be a wash, and the union between county and city police dissolved. Despite the breakup, the antique police cars remain as important historical artifacts of the police department's history.

28 JUNK FISH

Who is making those weird and wonderful fish?

They say one man's junk is another man's treasure, and that adage couldn't be truer for folk artist Ralph Douglas Jones. He is the founder of Fish Art Gallerie on Tybee Island and has been making whimsical creations out of reclaimed objects for more than twenty years.

Jones was originally a sign painter until he tried his hand at art to get himself out of a deep depression. His first sculpture was of a neon-lit fish titled *Lady in Red,* and the experience of creation had such a profound effect on him that he decided to make fish art from then on. Jones considers himself a "World Famous Artist" and has become famous with his signature Happy Fish designs. In a *Savannah Morning News* article, Jones described his inspiration as "the God spark." He was quoted as saying, "I lay a board on a table, and the fish creates itself. I'm sort of like the instrument creating the pieces."

Jones has made tens of thousands of unique pieces of art out of the junk he picks up at Goodwills, yard sales, or on the side of the road. His brightly colored fish are made out of everything from drift wood, metal roofing, and belt buckles to jewelry and washing machine parts. He can't seem to help himself—everything he looks at

---

Jones used to travel in and sell art
out of a psychedelic school bus.

Left, *A lot of shelf space is also devoted to healing crystals and other magical minerals.* Right, *Artist Ralph Douglas Jones has an infectious laugh that seems to come out in his happy fish.*

FISH ART GALLERIE

WHAT: A funky open-air, scrap-metal art gallery

WHERE: 1209 US-80 B, Tybee Island, GA 31328

COST: The art pieces are relatively inexpensive.

PRO TIP: $1 donation to take pictures

resembles a fish. When he needs a break from fish, Jones creates water fountains out of brass instruments and giant creatures, such as giraffes, mermaids, and dragons, out of welded metal.

Besides Jones' fish, visitors can purchase everything from jewelry to concert posters to bottle openers. Fish Art Gallerie is hard to miss when you are entering Tybee Island, with its piles of beautiful "junk" and colorful sculptures.

29 THE EARTHWORKS FORT

How did the Confederacy stop Union Naval ships from taking Savannah?

Brick-and-mortar forts are impressive, but nothing stops a cannonball like a mound of dirt. That's what Fort McAllister proved when it defended Savannah seven times against attacking ships sailing up the Ogeechee River.

Fort McAllister, in Bryan County, was built on a bluff called Genesis Point overlooking a bend in the Ogeechee River. Landowner Joseph McAllister pitched the idea to the Confederacy that if they built some earthwork forts and placed a few cannons at this critical spot they could successfully keep ships from using the river to invade Savannah, whose port was crucial to the Confederacy for trade with Europe.

Sure enough, when Union ships tried to pass, they got pushed back by Fort McAllister's cannon barrage. The Union upped the ante by sending their toughest weapon, the *Montauk* ironclad warship. Ironclads were making short work of wooden ships at sea, but the *Montauk* met its match against land-based defenses. For five hours, the *Montauk* blasted Fort McAllister with 15-inch cannons—the largest used in the war—without causing any casualties or damage to the earthworks. On the other hand, Fort McAllister's artillery made sixty-three direct

General Sherman was so angry that Confederate Major Anderson had laid mines around the fort that he made him join the enlisted men to dig them up.

No ships, even ironclads, were getting past this vantage point.

FORT MCALLISTER STATE PARK

WHAT: A dirt fort unconquerable by river

WHERE: 3894 Fort McAllister Road, Richmond Hill, GA 31324

COST: $5 Parking

PRO TIP: The state park includes campgrounds and seven cottages.

hits on the *Montauk* without causing a scratch to the iron hull. It wasn't until later, when General Sherman took the fort by land, that Fort McAllister fell and Savannah along with it, ending Sherman's "March to the Sea."

In 1930, Henry Ford used historic photos taken by Civil War photographer Samuel Cooley during the dismantling of the fort to accurately reconstruct Fort McAllister, and today it is a beautiful state park.

JUST A CASUAL STROLL

Who is the statue walking with an alligator?

Hilton Head Island, South Carolina, is a premier resort destination for golf and nature lovers, but if things had turned out differently, it could have been stripped of its beautiful trees for lumber. That was certainly the intention when Charles Fraser was sent there by his family lumber business to start chopping. At the time, only about 500 people lived on the island—mostly farmers and oyster workers. Fraser was so taken in by the natural grandeur of Hilton Head that he asked his father to grant him control of the island so that he could develop real estate on it.

After finishing Yale Law School, Fraser founded Sea Pines Company and began building world-renowned golf resorts and communities on Hilton Head. Because of his love for the trees that he was originally supposed to cut down, Fraser drafted covenants and restrictions to not only protect the trees but also make them the focus of development. Homes had to be neutral colors so that they wouldn't stand out among the trees. Winding roads and bike paths drew attention to the trees instead of the buildings. Strict rules were also set limiting the size of trees that could be removed from a homeowner's property.

CHARLES FRASER STATUE WITH AN ALLIGATOR

WHAT: A charming likeness of Hilton Head's mastermind

WHERE: Compass Rose Park, 4 St. Augustine Place, Hilton Head, SC

COST: Free

NOTEWORTHY: Fraser died in 2002 when his 28-foot *Sun Dance* yacht exploded and threw him, his wife, his daughter, and others into the water, where he drowned.

It is unclear what the leash laws are in Hilton Head, but this must be breaking some kind of regulation.

In 2011, to honor Fraser's role in building Hilton Head, a pair of sculptures were unveiled in Compass Rose Park depicting Fraser casually strolling alongside an alligator. The reference for this unusual pairing was from a photo published in 1962 in the *Saturday Evening Post* for a feature about Sea Pines. In the photo, Fraser, who was thirty-two at the time, was captured happily walking with an alligator while showing off his new development. Fraser's legacy as a tree-hugging real estate mogul is set in bronze.

Nobody knows what happened to the gator.

31

SPIRITS OF THE TREES

Where can you find the tree spirits of St. Simons Island?

Hidden all over St. Simons Island are more than twenty magical oak trees with somber, ghostly faces peering out from their bark. Local legend says that the faces represent the many sailors who died at sea while working on ships built from timber produced by St. Simons' lumber industry. Considering the serene, slumbering expressions on the peculiar trees, it's an easy tale to get caught up in.

The so-called tree spirits were actually carved by local artist Keith Jennings in the 1980s. Jennings began his work as a hobby in his backyard, but he was soon commissioned to carve his creations all over the island. Jennings usually took about two to four days to carve a face, but he doesn't take full credit for their appearance. Jennings believes that each tree reveals its spirit to him when carving. He has been quoted as saying, "I don't have that much to do with it. The wood speaks to you, ya know."

Although some of the tree spirits are on private property, visitors are encouraged to hunt around the island for as many carvings as they can find. To make it easier, the tree spirits are marked on GPS, and hunting maps can be downloaded from various websites, but that

---

Artist Keith Jennings also created the Mama Whale & Baby sculpture by the St. Simon Lighthouse.

Top, *This beautiful, hand-carved mermaid is the first spirit visitors should encounter when they begin their hunt for the other carvings around the island.* Bottom, *Those shooting hoops at one public basketball court have a permanent spectator in this wise, old tree spirit.*

ST. SIMONS ISLAND TREE SPIRITS

WHAT: Evocative tree carvings

WHERE: All over St. Simon's Island, GA

COST: Free

PRO TIP: The Golden Isles Welcome Center at 529 Beachview Drive has the first Tree Spirit and a map to find the others.

would take away from the unearthly thrill of stumbling across one of these mystical forest denizens while exploring the island. If you listen hard enough, maybe you can hear the spirits call to you through the rustle of their leaves in the coastal breeze.

32

CAN YOU HEAR ME NOW?

How does Jekyll Island fit into the first transcontinental phone call?

Everyone is familiar with Alexander Graham Bell's invention of the telephone as well as his historic first words. Few, however, recall that Bell was also present for another milestone in telecommunications when he participated in what could perhaps be called one of the first "conference calls," one that connected him to various cities across the country and also Jekyll Island, Georgia.

On January 25, 1915, Theodore N. Vail, the first president of AT&T, took part in the very first transcontinental phone call from the Jekyll Island Club, connecting him with Alexander Graham Bell in New York City; Bell's assistant, Thomas Watson, in San Francisco; and President Woodrow Wilson at the White House in Washington, D.C.

It was a massive undertaking, with 130,000 telephone poles running four copper wires from coast to coast and 1,500 AT&T employees stationed along the entire line to make sure nothing went wrong. The conversation was a success, and the participants even had a little fun when Bell was coaxed into repeating his famous line, "Mr. Watson, come here please. I want you." Watson responded from San Fransisco that it would take him a week to get to New York. The conversation ended when

---

The Jekyll Island Club was the gathering spot for the wealthiest men in America, including Rockefeller, the Vanderbilts, and the Morgans.

A museum dedicated to the island features a recreation of the significant phone call.

President Wilson finally got on the line and congratulated Vail for achieving this amazing feat.

In 1965, to commemorate the fiftieth anniversary of the first transcontinental phone call, the Georgia Chapter of the Telephone Pioneers of America (an organization founded by Vail in 1911) erected a monument featuring an old telephone similar to the one used in 1915 in a glass case near Indian Mound Cottage on Jekyll Island.

FIRST TRANSCONTINENTAL PHONE CALL MONUMENT

WHAT: An old phone commemorating a milestone in telecommunications

WHERE: Riverview Drive near the Jekyll Island Club, Jekyll Island, GA

COST: Free to look at the phone

NOTEWORTHY: The Jekyll Island Club was also the birthplace of the Federal Reserve System.

33

DEVILS ON WHEELS

Who are Savannah's fiery roller derby divas?

It's hard to imagine that roller derby—the on-again, off-again underground woman's contact sport—has been around since the early 1900s. It began as banked track racing, with teams sometimes competing in 3,000-mile marathons called "transcontinental roller derby." After a hiatus during World War II, roller derby returned in a more aggressive, over-the-top form in the 1940s, with loosely scripted storylines and an emphasis on theatrics over athletics—think professional wrestling on tiny wheels.

By the end of the 1970s, roller derby had largely faded away, but in the early 2000s grassroots efforts brought it back. With leagues and teams suddenly sprouting up across the country, Savannah wanted to get in on the action. In 2006, Heather Hamilton Watson, known in roller derby as Ms. Dfiant, invited women to Star Castle Family Entertainment Center to try to put a team together. Many who showed up hadn't skated in years, and none had ever seen an actual derby, but like a moment out of a scrappy, underdog sports movie, the Savannah Derby Devils were born.

By 2014, the Derby Devils had become full members of the Woman's Flat Track Derby Association (WFTDA) and had put together a committed, hard-working team of amazing women. Although modern roller derby has

---

Besides skating in the rink, the Derby Devils also participate in community service projects.

Derbies can be as thrilling as a pro wrestling match—even without the theatrics. (Photos by Casey Jones.)

THE SAVANNAH DERBY DEVILS

WHAT: Savannah's Roller Derby Queens

WHERE: Home games are at Savannah Convention Center, 1 International Drive, Savannah, GA

COST: $12 adults, $2 children

PRO TIP: Check out the schedule of events at savannahderby.com.

dropped the theatrics and is treated like a legitimate sport (with attempts to even get it into the Olympics), the "jammers" and "blockers" still retain their wild names and tough, colorful personas. Like superheroes, the Savannah Derby Devils are an inspiration to women and young girls in Savannah. There is even a "little sister" league for girls ages eight to seventeen called the Savannah Jr. Derbytaunts.

34 THE SLOTH OF SKIDAWAY

Where can you see the skeleton of a 20-foot megafauna?

With its maritime forest and salt marsh, Skidaway Island National Park can feel like a prehistoric jungle from *The Lost World*. While strolling along its winding trails, one could easily envision a duck-billed Hadrosaurid slowly poking its head out from the damp brush. If you can't help imagining dinosaurs wandering the island's woods, then you may be delighted to meet one of the actual giants that lived in these parts not too long ago (geologically speaking).

Inside the park's interpretive center, among taxidermied animals, bird-watching stations, and reptile tanks, stands a towering example of Savannah's prehistoric wildlife. One of the island's earliest inhabitants was the Eremotherium, or giant ground sloth, which roamed the Savannah area more than 10,000 years ago. This ice-age herbivore stood twenty feet tall, weighed three to five tons, and is a cousin to the smaller sloths currently living in the rain forests of Central and South America.

The first giant sloth found in North America was actually dug up on Skidaway Island in the early 1800s, which greatly surprised the scientific community because up until that moment, it was believed that the giant sloth lived only

GIANT SLOTH SKELETON

WHAT: A replica of the one of Savannah's earliest inhabitants

WHERE: Skidaway Island National Park, 52 Diamond Causeway, Savannah, GA

COST: $5 parking

PRO TIP: After visiting the sloth, walk the park's trails to see an old moonshining still from the Prohibition era.

Left, *With its massive claws, the giant sloth may look menacing, but if it was as slow as its modern cousin then early man had nothing to worry about. (Courtesy of Skidaway Island State Park.)* Above, *This illustration depicts how massive the gentle sloths were compared to humans. (Courtesy of Skidaway Island State Park.)*

in South America. After inhabiting Savannah for more than two million years, no one is sure why they eventually disappeared. Was it climate change, or were they hunted to extinction by Paleo-Indians? That would have been one impressive steak!

A replica skeleton of this imposing creature was set up in the interpretive center as a hulking example of the wide variety of life that has existed in Southeast Georgia.

The skeleton is an exact replica of the giant sloth in the Smithsonian's Natural History Museum.

35

CALL OF THE WILD

Where can you meet a pack of grey wolves?

Savannah may not have a proper zoo, but there is one place where you can see more than 100 different animals native to Georgia. Oatland Island Wildlife Center has been operating since 1973, educating area students and visitors about Savannah's salt marsh ecosystem. Built in 1927, the main building was originally a retirement home for the Order of Railroad Conductors. Then from World War II until the 1970s, Oatland Island was used as a research facility for everything from sexually transmitted diseases and leprosy to malaria and the banned pesticide DDT until it was purchased by the Savannah-Chatham County Public School System.

Now, as you hike the more than two-mile-long trail, you can see various birds of prey, bobcats, foxes, alligators, snakes, flying squirrels, bison, armadillos, tortoises, cougars, and farm animals, but the real stars of the wildlife center are the non-native species on display.

The end of the trail leads visitors into an area called Wolf Wilderness, where a pack of grey wolves resides. An air-conditioned building with a glass wall allows visitors to safely observe the wolf pack as they eat, play, and generally lope around the enclosure. The wolves are a

In 2018, Oatland Island was hit by a devastating tornado. None of the people or animals were harmed, but the center was closed for months for repairs.

Left, *One of the pack cools off by the water on a hot summer day.* Right, *The No-Pest fly strip was invented at Oatland Island during its days as a research facility.*

favorite exhibit of Oatland Island, and it's always a highlight when visitors can hear the forlorn howling of the pack from anywhere in the park.

In 2016, four new wolf pups were added to replenish the pack. They were named after rivers of Georgia—Oconee, Suwanee, Satilla, and Ogeechee—and in a naming ceremony the pups had the opportunity to choose their own name by digging into one of four boxes of food and confetti, each labeled with a different name. It was pretty cute.

OATLAND ISLAND'S GREY WOLF PACK

WHAT: The only wolves you'll find in Southeast Georgia

WHERE: Oatland Island Wildlife Center, 711 Sandtown Road, Savannah, GA

COST: $5 adults, $3 children

PRO TIP: Children will love the annual events, such as the Gnome & Fairy Festival and the Sheep to Shawl.

36

KEHOE HOUSE DISCO

Which historic mansion was almost turned into a nightclub?

Built in 1893 by architect Dewitt Bruyn for William Kehoe, a successful local iron foundry owner, the Kehoe House is easily one the most impressive mansions in Savannah. The dark red brick home was built in the Queen Anne Revival style and was massive enough to comfortably accommodate Kehoe's large family—he had many children, ten of whom survived. One of the most unique features of the house is its decorative exterior stairways, balustrades, window treatments, fluted columns and capitals, fences and gates, all of which were made out of cast iron instead of wood to show off the skill of ironworking Kehoe's foundry produced.

Over the years, the Kehoe House changed ownership several times. For most of the twentieth century, it was a mortuary, which means several stories of hauntings are attached to it. Then it was briefly a private residence. After that is where the home's history gets a little unusual (ghost stories not withstanding).

In the 1980s, football Hall of Famer Joe Namath bought the house for $80,000. It should be noted for this story that back in 1969, just months after winning Super Bowl III, Namath tearfully announced his retirement from

---

The Kehoe House was once home to Goette Funeral Home, which means it also has a haunted reputation.

What Namath saw in this imposing mansion to make him think, "dance club," is anyone's guess.

THE KEHOE HOUSE BED & BREAKFAST

WHAT: The Joe Namath-owned disco that almost was

WHERE: 123 Habersham Street, Savannah, GA

COST: Check for rates

PRO TIP: The Bed and Breakfast is for adults only, which is in keeping with its nearly a nightclub past.

football because he didn't want to give up his stake in his New York singles bar, Bachelors III. A few months later he relented, sold his share of the bar, and returned to football. Namath's love of the nightlife apparently never wained, however, and his intention was to turn the majestic Kehoe House into a nightclub/disco. Of course, the other residents of Columbia Square wouldn't have it, so he dropped the idea and eventually resold the house for $530,000.

Today, the Kehoe House is a luxurious Bed and Breakfast, but if you stay there, close your eyes and try to picture what it would have looked like with strobe lights, disco balls, a DJ booth, and people lining the block around the square waiting to get turned away by a bouncer.

37

THE GIRL WHO WAVED

Who was the amazing woman who welcomed ships to Savannah?

For many kindhearted human beings, the impulse to throw a friendly wave to passing ships is pretty strong, but one local Savannah woman made it her unofficial lifelong duty.

Florence Martus was known to Savannahians and sailors around the world as the waving girl. Born in 1868, Florence was the daughter of a sergeant stationed at Fort Pulaski. As a teenager, Florence moved into a remote cottage on the bank of the Savannah River with her brother, George, a lighthouse keeper who had been transferred from Cockspur Island Lighthouse to Elba Island Lighthouse, where they lived a rather lonely and solitary life.

From an early age, Florence had waved to ships as they entered Savannah Harbor, and that habit became a personal duty by the time she moved onto Elba Island. With her loyal collie by her side, Florence would greet every passing ship with a wave of her handkerchief during the day and a lantern at night. The ships would return the greeting with a blast of their horn, and her reputation began to spread among sailors everywhere. This tradition continued for forty-four years, and by the time she stopped in 1931, it was estimated that Florence had waved to more than 50,000 ships without missing

---

Artist Felix De Weldon also created the Iwo Jima Monument.

Florence Martus continues to wave to several cargo ships a day.

one. Local lore suggests that Florence waved to every ship in the hopes that the sailor she had fallen in love with when she was young would return. More likely, she just enjoyed the attention and gifts from the sailors.

In 1943, a Liberty ship built in Savannah was named the *SS Florence Martus* in her honor. A statue of Florence Martus, sculpted by famed artist Felix De Weldon, was erected on River Street. Facing the river, the statue depicts Florence waving her handkerchief with her dog by her side so that the waving girl can continue the tradition of welcoming ships to Savannah.

38

GOT MAIL?

Why is there a giant mailbox on Quacco Road?

Towering over a cattle farm on Quacco Road is a gigantic 16-foot mailbox standing on a 20-foot pole. The massive mailbox, painted black and white like a cow, has a knack for slowing down passing traffic. Families regularly stop on the side of the road to take pictures of the unusual landmark.

The oddity was built by Charles Hubert Keller, former owner of Keller's Flea Market. Keller constructed the mailbox as a companion piece to the flea market's big bovine mascot, Kelly the Cow, but according to Keller, his wife didn't want the popular cow to be upstaged. Instead, Keller set up the mailbox in front of his farm and jokes that he is "expecting a large check from the government."

Keller has built all kinds of unusual creations that can be found scattered around his farm, including a couch made out of a clawfoot tub, a pirate ship and a comically oversized lounge chair that he enters in parades, and a functional six-person motorcycle. Keller's main passion is racing, and he enjoys building bizarre vehicles, such as a car straight out of *Mad Max* that is covered in skulls, has a coffin with a skeleton in the back, and shoots large bursts of flame out of its two vertical exhaust pipes.

GIANT MAILBOX

WHAT: A quirky companion piece to Keller's giant cow

WHERE: 1017 Quacco Road, Savannah, GA

COST: Free

PRO TIP: If you get a chance to meet Keller, ask him to show you some of his other crazy creations.

Is it possible that Kelly the Keller's Flea Market cow gets her fan mail delivered here?

Keller will probably never get that giant check he's waiting for, but maybe someday he will at least receive some jumbo-sized fan mail for his contributions to keeping Savannah eccentric.

The red flag on the side is upright, suggesting that it contains some outgoing mail, but it's difficult to imagine how the mailman is going to retrieve it.

39 SAY A "LITTLE" PRAYER

Does Townsend, Georgia, have the smallest church in America?

We all have dreams and goals in life, but not everyone gets to see them realized. One Georgian who did see her humble dream come to fruition was Agnes Harper, a local grocer, who in 1949 oversaw the construction of Christ Chapel Church, more commonly known as "the smallest church in America."

Whether or not Christ Chapel Church is actually the smallest church in America is up for debate, but that doesn't take away from its quaint charms. The tiny 10 × 15-foot building was designed by Harper to be a refuge and place of meditation for weary travelers. It may be small, but the church has all the necessary features you would expect to find in a larger church. There is a pulpit, a dozen chairs (in lieu of pews), stained-glass windows imported from England, and even a small-scale bell tower outside.

In 2015, Christ Chapel Church was vandalized by fire. Apparently, someone tried to use a torch to break open

---

The church was built with private funds, but according to Harper's wishes, the deed is made out to Jesus Christ.

Left, *The Christ Church Chapel looks good as new after being rebuilt following its destruction in a fire.* Right, *The humble church has everything a house of worship needs, all in a tiny space.*

the donation box and ended up burning down the church instead. Donations and help immediately began pouring in the day after to restore the beloved landmark. Thanks to the hard work of volunteers, Christ Chapel Church was restored to its former glory eighteen months later and continues to receive daily visitors.

CHRIST CHURCH CHAPEL

WHAT: A small church built from big hearts

WHERE: US HWY 17 South, I-95 Exit 67, Townsend, GA

COST: Free, but donations are welcome

PRO TIP: Although it doesn't fit many congregants, the church offers nondenominational services every third Sunday.

40 THE BENCH

Where is Forrest Gump's bench?

Although it's not exactly a secret, this author would be remiss if he didn't include Forrest Gump's bench in the pages of this book. "Where is the bench?" is the most common question uttered by Savannah tourists. Forget General Oglethorpe. Forget Mary Telfair. People want to know about Forrest Gump and, hopefully, this will be this author's last word on the subject.

Released in 1994 and starring Tom Hanks, "America's Dad," the incredibly popular *Forrest Gump* went on to win several Academy Awards, including Best Picture, Best Actor, Best Director, Best Adapted Screenplay, and Best Visual Effects. *Forrest Gump* was shot primarily in Savannah, and the most prominent location was a "bus stop" on Chippewa Square. The framing device of the film has Forrest waiting for the bus on a bench, where he recounts his entire life story to strangers who sit next to him.

The first bit of news that never fails to disappoint visitors is that the bench was merely a movie prop and taken away as soon as filming wrapped up. Forrest Gump's bench can be seen in the Savannah Visitor Center, but it's actually a replica (the original is in a Paramount warehouse), adding further disappointment.

In the opening scene of the movie, a feather can be seen fluttering past the Independent Presbyterian Church across the street.

FORREST GUMP BENCH LOCATION

WHAT: The site of a favorite, iconic cinematic moment

WHERE: Chippewa Square, Savannah, GA

COST: Free

NOTEWORTHY: Eagle-eyed viewers of the film may notice that traffic, which normally runs counterclockwise around the square, is going in the wrong direction. This was necessary for the filmmakers to do so that the bus's door could open on the correct side.

Plants now grow where the bench once sat, making it difficult for visitors to identify where Forrest Gump waited for the bus.

If you want to visit the actual film location of the famous scene, it is on the north side of Chippewa Square, with the statue of Oglethorpe facing away. For the film, a brick platform was placed on the ground by Hull Street for the bench to stand on, but now there is a flower bed and street sign. It is probably for the best that the bench isn't actually there because the constant queue of people posing for photos with boxes of chocolate in hand would definitely slow down traffic.

41 THE PRESIDENTIAL DIVE BAR

Which Savannah bar was frequented by President Jimmy Carter?

The plastic Pabst Blue Ribbon sign that hangs outside of Pinkie Master's, Savannah's iconic neighborhood corner dive bar, is a glowing beacon that draws thirsty patrons in like moths. One of its most famous patrons has a bit of political history tied to this popular establishment.

Pinkie Master's was opened in 1953 by Luis Christopher Masterpolis, better known as Pinkie. Being politically minded, Pinkie was an early supporter of Jimmy Carter, and consequently Carter visited Pinkie's bar on several occasions while campaigning as a state senator and Georgia governor. The popular story is that Carter even announced his run for president from the bar at Pinkie's. This story is probably not entirely true, but Carter did stand on the bar on another occasion.

Pinkie passed away after Carter was elected president, so when Carter visited Savannah on St. Patrick's Day in 1978, he snuck out of the Desoto Hilton Hotel with his security detail and stopped in at Pinkie Master's.

JIMMY CARTER PLAQUE AT PINKIE MASTER'S

WHAT: The commemoration of a U.S. President's favorite Savannah bar

WHERE: The Original Pinkie Masters, 318 Drayton Street, Savannah, GA

COST: The price of a drink

PRO TIP: Pinkie's is cash only, but the drinks are inexpensive.

Left, *The ownership of Pinkie's may change, but the clientele never does.*
Right, *Pinkies has one of the best jukebox selections in the city.*

There Carter stood on the bar and addressed the people present with a fond tribute to his good friend Pinkie. To commemorate the moment, a plaque was placed on the bar where Carter stood.

Pinkie Master's changed owners several times over the years, and when a former owner was ignominiously evicted from the building, he took the plaque with him. Fortunately, a year later, the plaque was returned to its rightful home. On St. Patrick's Day 2017, a ceremony was held at what is now called The Original Pinkie Master's to set the plaque back into the bar. Former President Jimmy Carter even sent a signed letter of support that

This is the bar on which a sitting president stood.

read, "I will always remember the times I had at your establishment. When I ran for Governor, Pinkie himself was one of my most important supporters. And when I was back in Savannah as President of the United States, I will never forget standing on the bar to say thank you."

The previous owner of Pinkie's tried to reopen his version near River Street, so for a while there were dueling Pinkie Masters bars.

Pinkie's long history can be traced on its walls through old photographs and quirky art work.

A FACE ON THE WALL (page 50)

CAPTAIN FLINT'S LAST STOP (page 202)

CAN YOU HEAR ME NOW? (page 64)

TREASURE ISLAND? (page 52)

PLANET OF THE GEEKS (page 48)

WHAT'S THE PASSWORD? (page 44)

Large cast iron store lifter, advertising premium, Art Stove Company, Detroit, Cut Out The Whiskey, 1912.

JUNK FISH (page 56)

SAVANNAH'S ST. BERNADETTE (page 26)

DEVILS ON WHEELS (page 66)

Photo by Casey Jones

RARE READS (page 198)

THE HEARTBROKEN GIRL (page 124)

AN OUTSIDER'S MEMORIAL

Why did an outsider artist construct a Black Holocaust Memorial?

In 2002, the controversial African-American Family Monument statue was unveiled on River Street. Some residents of Savannah were dismayed by the confusing message being sent by the monument. Its original intention was to draw attention to the many families that suffered during the slave trade, but higher-ups decided that the image should be softened since it would be in such a prominent spot on River Street, and they didn't want to upset tourists. The statue, sculpted by a white woman, depicts a well-dressed African-American family with chains at their feet, and most people struggle to understand what exactly it all symbolizes.

One local artist was so disappointed with the statue that he took it upon himself to construct a proper, unflinching memorial to the suffering of slaves. In 2004, Jimmy "Double Dutch" Kimble built his Black Holocaust Memorial behind his home at Anderson and East Broad Streets. Constructed out of papier-mâché, Kimble's Black Holocaust Memorial depicts a black man in a loin cloth and chains flanked by a woman and two children. Next to

THE BLACK HOLOCAUST MEMORIAL

WHAT: A passionate artistic statement by a singular folk artist

WHERE: East Anderson Lane, Savannah, GA 31401

COST: Free

PRO TIP: The easiest way to get to the Black Holocaust Memorial is to drive northbound up one-way East Broad Street and turn left into the lane.

Kimble's back yard is his art gallery.

the sculpture is a ferocious image of a black panther with the words "New Black Panther Party" above it. Kimble was worried that the black children in his neighborhood were not learning the truth about slavery—particularly from wishy-washy images, such as the River Street monument—and wanted to educate them about the slaves who died for their freedom. The sculpture is also meant to teach children that they will be put in chains if they get into trouble and have the police put handcuffs on them.

Kimble received recognition for his achievement from several politicians, including Rep. Craig Gordon of the Georgia House of Representatives.

In a city full of monuments, Kimble's may be the most personal.

Despite the intense imagery of the Black Holocaust Memorial, Kimble is a warmhearted man who loves children and is always available to meet and talk with visitors. Kimble has built upon his sculpture with more many more whimsical pieces depicting animals and cartoons, such as characters from the animated film *Madagascar*. Children are always invited to hang out at his place and play or fix their bicycles with his tools, and he even hosts annual Christmas and Halloween gatherings for the neighborhood. Kimble and his incredible art are a shining example of the power of creativity and its impact on the community.

Above, *Some pieces are fun and silly, but many are powerful and fierce.* Right, *The figure of an enchained slave is meant to depict the harsh reality of the American slave trade to the neighborhood's young residents.*

43

SAVANNAH UNDERGROUND

Are tunnels hidden underneath Savannah?

History, rumor, and tall tales become a labyrinthine tangle of misinformation regarding the network of tunnels that run beneath Savannah. Most people have never actually seen the tunnels for themselves, and tour guides, historians, and city workers all have conflicting ideas about what tunnels run where and what was transported through them.

The Pirate's House Restaurant, for example, purports that the tunnel underneath its establishment was once used to "shanghai" drunken sailors. The stories suggest that either pirates or merely unscrupulous ship captains looking to forcefully volunteer sailors into their crew dragged victims down to the rum cellar and then to the river through a secret tunnel. Considering that most of the fantastic pirate stories tied to the restaurant were likely made up by its owners, the tunnel probably wasn't used for such nefarious purposes.

There are rumors that tunnels under the city were used for transporting slaves to auctions in Wright Square to avoid having to parade them through the city streets. Another rumor related to the slave trade is that the cellar under the First African Baptist Church was used as an underground railroad, which is likely true because air holes shaped like African prayer symbols can be found in the floors below the church. Like most of the history of Savannah's tunnels, these stories remain obfuscated and unconfirmed.

Savannah knows its history, but in the case of the city's tunnels, there are more rumors than answers.

The entrance to the Candler Hospital morgue tunnel can be found through these doors.

SAVANNAH TUNNELS

WHAT: Secret tunnels, cellars, and passageways that lie under the city

WHERE: All over Savannah

COST: N/A

PRO TIP: Almost all of the tunnels are sealed, but many tours will show you where they are supposedly located.

One of the most popular legends about Savannah's tunnels involves the yellow fever epidemic of 1876. Many believe that so many people were dying at Candler Hospital from yellow fever that tunnels were built under Forsyth Park to hide the bodies and prevent mass hysteria. Although there is a tunnel that runs from the site of the old Candler Hospital under Drayton Street, it was actually constructed in 1884, eight years after the epidemic. The true purpose of the tunnel was to move the morgue, or "dead house," from out of the building to underground.

Although there are mysterious tunnels and cellars all over the city, the history of most of them has been lost to time, and investigations only lead to literal and metaphorical dead ends. The stories are still captivating, though, and continue to be a large part of Savannah's mystique.

44

GALLERY OF DRUNKEN NAPKIN ART

Which bar boasts a large collection of Abraham Lincoln portraits?

Anyone who says they can't draw just needs a stiff drink, a pen, and a paper napkin to unlock the hidden creative potential they never knew they had. The humble napkin drawing is a great artistic equalizer, with even the most rudimentary scribbles having some charming aspects. Abe's on Lincoln, a bar located in Savannah's Historic District, has taken the idea of the napkin drawing and elevated it into a sort of communal art installation.

Abe's on Lincoln is the latest name of one of the oldest continuously running bars in the city, which has been around since the late 1700s. The bar has gone through many identities, but Abe's takes its name from the street it's located on—Lincoln Street.

The interior of Abe's is covered with napkin drawings on almost every available piece of wall and ceiling. All of the drawings share the same subject—Abraham Lincoln. The tradition of drawing a portrait of Lincoln began years ago when a drunk man came into the bar but couldn't afford a drink. Instead, he asked the bartender for a napkin and pen and proceeded to draw a striking portrait

---

Lincoln Street was named after Benjamin Lincoln, a Revolutionary War hero, rather than the sixteenth president of the United States.

Above, *The bar at the corner of Lincoln Street has been there for a long time, and it shows.* Right, *It doesn't take a lot of talent to have your work hung in one of the strangest art galleries in the city.*

of Abraham Lincoln that the bartender enjoyed so much he hung it on the wall for posterity. Soon after, other patrons tried their hand at drawing Lincoln, and countless representations have adorned the walls ever since.

The depictions of Lincoln vary from surprisingly realistic to simple and silly. There are zombie Lincolns, SpongeBob Lincolns, hipster Lincolns, drag queen Lincolns, and your standard top hat-wearing Lincolns. The only rules that apply if you want your drawing hung up are that they can't have racist, bigoted, or sexist imagery, they should be signed and dated, and they should show some effort—if you do stick figures, they better be pretty good stick figures.

ABE'S ON LINCOLN

WHAT: A gallery of unique napkin art

WHERE: 17 Lincoln Street, Savannah, GA 31401

COST: The drinks aren't free, but the napkins are.

PRO TIP: Bring your favorite pen.

45 CHAD'S MAGIC TREEHOUSE

Where can you spend the night in a treehouse?

Many quaint inns and luxurious hotels are available to stay in during a visit to Savannah, but none are as unique as Diamond Oaks Treehouse Suite. Diamond Oaks is the home of local poet and author Chad Faries. Those who have read Chad's wild memoir *Drive Me Out of My Mind* will immediately understand why he created such a magical space for himself—his nomadic lifestyle as a child had him living in twenty-four different houses in ten years!

Chad's desire to settle into a permanent home led him to Savannah and this little cottage under a forlorn oak tree in the little fishing village of Thunderbolt. With the help of his friends from the literary world, Chad took the fixer-upper and transformed it into a dream home tailored to his Peter Pan personality. It would take too long to describe every amusing detail of his home (such as the nooks for his motorcycle helmet and cowboy boot collections), but the standout features are his bedroom suite and treehouse. The bedroom is built in the converted attic and features six large skylights that allow you to stargaze while you

DIAMOND OAKS TREEHOUSE SKYLIGHT SUITE

WHAT: A "diamond" in the rough when it comes to B&Bs

WHERE: 10 Bonaventure Road, Thunderbolt, GA 31404

COST: $120 a night

PRO TIP: The suite can be booked on Airbnb. Try reading Chad's book before you see his house to get some insight into why he put so much work into it.

Left, *Diamond Oaks is three floors of magical whimsy—four if you count the treehouse. (Photo by Geoff Johnson.)* Right, *Even the treehouse is full of little creative touches that make this one of the most unique houses in Savannah. (Photo by Geoff Johnson.)*

drift away to sleep. The treehouse set atop the oak tree is a marvel, with such romantic touches as a suspended bed, a chandelier, and a pulley for hoisting up food and champagne. Many newlyweds have spent the night under its branches.

Diamond Oaks has been featured in *Savannah Magazine*, *Glamour*, and *This Old House*, and is considered by many Savannahians to be their favorite house anywhere. Diamond Oak Treehouse suite as well as the parlor room are available for rent on Airbnb and is close to both downtown and Bonaventure Cemetery. It is an ideal hideaway from the usual bustle of hotels.

Novelist Adam Davies and "The Moth" founder George Dawes Greene lent their muscle to help restore the house.

THE HAUNTED "BOO-ERY"

What is the most paranormal place in Savannah?

Savannah holds a reputation for being the most haunted city in America—a distinction it was given by the American Institute of Paranormal Activity in 2003. Of all the haunted spaces in Savannah, Moon River Brewing Company is hands down the most supernaturally active.

Moon River opened its brewery and restaurant in 1999 in the location of the old City Hotel. Built in 1821, the City Hotel was Savannah's first hotel. It being an old building, many historically documented occurrences lend fuel to Moon River's many ghost sightings. One of the most notable is the story of the feud between a gambler and a doctor that led to murder.

In 1832, a local miscreant named James Stark had sparked an ongoing feud with a physician named Dr. Phillip Minis. One day while getting drunk in the City Hotel bar, Stark said some nasty things about Minis, so naturally the good doctor shot him on the spot. Fortunately for Dr. Minis, nobody seemed to like Stark, so he was acquitted for murder and able to continue practicing medicine.

The City Hotel shut down permanently when General Sherman and the Union Army showed up, and the building wasn't really used for much else until its

Moon River's building was also the home of the first branch of the U.S. Post Office in Savannah.

114

Left, *Moon River added a dog-friendly beer garden in 2013, which is probably the least haunted area in the establishment.* Right, *Most of the scariest ghost encounters happen upstairs.*

MOON RIVER BREWING COMPANY

WHAT: The most paranormally active place in Savannah

WHERE: 21 West Bay Street, Savannah, GA

COST: Varies

PRO TIP: Several ghost tour companies make regular stops at Moon River, so ask ahead before you book a tour.

renovation by Moon River in the 1990s. After all that time, something must have knocked dormant spirits loose during renovation because paranormal activity is exceptionally high at the brewery. The staff and customers of Moon River have so many stories about shadow people, flying bottles, a pushy ghost named "Toby," and a frightening third floor that renovators refuse to finish. It was featured on both The Travel Channel's *Ghost Adventures* and SciFi Channel's *Ghost Hunters*.

Besides the hauntings, Moon River has an excellent selection of craft beers on tap, so come for the "Boo!" and stay for the brew.

47

THE CASTLE IN THE WOODS

Where is Savannah's old Powder Magazine?

Of all Savannah's historical buildings, the Savannah Powder Magazine remains its most secret and remote—and for good reason. The Powder Magazine was built in 1898 to house the city's supply of gunpowder and dynamite well away from populated areas so that if it accidentally blew up it wouldn't take half the city with it.

Mayor Peter Meldrim went all out and hired famous architects Alfred S. Eichberg and Hyman Witcover to design the magazine. Having designed City Hall and Telfair Hospital between them, Eichberg and Witcover were probably a little overqualified to build what basically amounted to a storage shed that no one was meant to see. Not content with building a brick box, the architects decided instead on Gothic, or King Arthur style, that resembles a medieval castle complete with parapets. The structure is considered the strongest in Savannah, with three-foot thick brick walls and a steel-reinforced roof to keep the explosive materials safe.

With the demand for explosives waining, the Powder Magazine closed in 1963 and remarkably has been abandoned ever since. There were several ideas for restoring it, including a failed attempt in the 1990s by local activist Tommy Holland to turn the area into a park,

---

The tar floors still show the imprints of the gunpowder barrels.

It may have seen better days, but the Powder Magazine could probably outlast every other building in Savannah.

THE POWDER MAGAZINE

WHAT: A hidden castle that housed explosives

WHERE: In the woods by Ogeechee Road near Chatham Parkway

COST: Free

PRO TIP: The Powder Magazine is popular with geocachers, so if you're having trouble finding it, follow the coordinates.

but mostly it had been used as shelter by the homeless. Attempts to preserve the Powder Magazine continue to this day, but any progress still seems a long time coming.

The Powder Magazine can be found off U.S. 17, east of Chatham Parkway, but it takes a little intrepid exploring through the woods to get to it. The entrances are currently boarded up, but since the building is on public property it's okay to visit it.

48

CINEMATIC TREATS

Where can you eat ice cream with Hollywood flair?

Film producer Stratton Leopold spent forty years making hit films in Hollywood, but in Savannah his name is more commonly associated with frozen desserts. Founded in 1919 by three Greek immigrant brothers, Leopold's Ice Cream quickly became a hot spot for cold treats. Originally located at the corner of Habersham and Gwinnett Streets, Leopold's became famous for their in-house made ice cream, particularly their signature Tutti Frutti flavor. Stratton grew up in the family business and eventually took over after his father passed away, but in 1969 he closed up shop to pursue his dream of making movies.

In 2004, Stratton and his wife returned to Savannah and reopened Leopold's Ice Cream in a new prime location on Broughton Street right next to Trustees Theater under the prominent SCAD sign. Fortunately, Stratton had kept most of the original features from the old shop, such as a black marble soda fountain, an old phone booth, and a wooden back bar, and incorporated them into the new design. The retro, throwback look of the shop was created by Academy Award–nominated set designer Dan Lomino and is the platonic ideal of a soda shop.

LEOPOLD'S ICE CREAM

WHAT: A movie mogul's sweet passion for the family business

WHERE: 212 East Broughton Street

COST: See menu

PRO TIP: If the line is too long for you, you can now order Leopold's ice cream online for delivery.

Old fashioned soda shops never go out of style.

Leopold's décor also features memorabilia from Stratton's decades as a successful producer in Hollywood. There is a film editing machine and movie camera and tripod. A glass display case contains props from such films as *The Sum of All Fears*. The walls are adorned with movie posters from such films as *Captain America: The First Avenger, Hamburger Hill, Paycheck,* and *Mission Impossible III*, as well as autographed photos of Stratton's actor friends, such as Ben Affleck, Morgan Freeman, and Bob Hope.

The lines may sometimes be long at Leopold's, but it's worth the wait to get a taste of Savannah and Hollywood history in one bite, and if you're lucky, you'll get to meet Stratton himself as he dips scoops for customers, just as he has since he was a child.

Stratton Leopold was Executive Vice President at Paramount Pictures.

49 FLYING FORTRESS

Where can you see a World War II-era B-17 bomber?

When cruising down I-95, drivers can catch a glimpse of some historic military planes, for example, a MiG 17-A or an F-4 Phantom II, parked in the grass outside a building. Those interested in airplanes or military history may want to pull off the highway and visit one of the most unforgettable museums in Georgia.

The National Mighty Eighth Museum in Pooler is the only museum in the world exclusively dedicated to preserving the stories of the Eighth Air Force, "the greatest air armada of all time." The museum features several exhibits devoted to recounting the various aspects of the Eighth's history, such as a look at the buildup to World War II told through the artifacts brought back by American soldiers after the war or the Mission Experience, which shows visitors what it was like to go on a bombing mission.

The Combat Gallery features a Boeing-Stearman PT-Kaydet, the nosepiece of a "Fightin' Sam" B-24 Liberator, and models of a P-51 Mustang and a German Messerschmidt Bf 109. The crown jewel of the museum, however, is the "City of Savannah," an actual B-17 Flying Fortress. The legendary B-17 was the most effective bomber used during World War II.

The "City of Savannah," named after the 5,000 combat aircraft to be processed at Hunter Airfield in Savannah during WWII, was donated by the Smithsonian Air and Space Museum in 2009 and has been an ongoing restoration project. The ultimate goal is to make it mission ready and the "finest static display of a B-17 in

Top, Volunteers have spent ten years restoring the City of Savannah, but there is still a lot they want to do, such as automating its three turrets. Bottom, The rotunda upon entering the building sets a suitable, reverent tone for the rest of the museum.

THE NATIONAL MIGHTY EIGHTH MUSEUM

WHAT: An almost fully restored B-17 bomber

WHERE: 175 Bourne Avenue, Pooler, GA 31322

COST: $8–$12

NOTEWORTHY: The museum has a research center with more than 10,000 books, diaries, and historical documents.

the world." Even with the restoration incomplete, it is still an impressive sight. The room barely contains the plane's massive wingspan, and it is the only B-17 that is open to the public. Visitors shouldn't miss the unique experience of entering and experiencing this singular aircraft.

Many volunteers at the museum are WWII Eighth Air Force veterans.

50

REALITY REALTY

Which Savannah home was the product of a popular reality show?

Back in 2010, ABC's *Extreme Makeover: Home Edition* was making American television audiences cry buckets of happy tears as they watched wholesome, deserving families get their dream homes. The show, hosted by hammer-wielding hunk Ty Pennington, was a huge hit, so when it was announced that they were filming an episode in Savannah, locals jumped for joy.

The Simpson family was chosen for the makeover treatment based on the medical condition of their youngest child and the overwhelmingly dilapidated state of the house they were unable to restore. (The author actually looked at this house while house shopping just before the Simpsons bought it and can attest to the unfixable condition it was in.) Hundreds of local volunteers worked around the clock for six days to construct the new home, and the final result was a cheerful, mint green neo-Victorian home with a therapy room and heated pool for their child's medical needs. It was another feel-good episode that certainly provoked a lot of crying. Unfortunately, as was common with many

---

The Simpsons also received a Ford Explorer, iPads, computers, and a lifetime family membership to the Telfair Museum of Art.

The designers looked to other notable homes in the area for inspiration. The circle patterns on the porch, for example, were influenced by Savannah's Historic Gingerbread House.

of the participants of *Extreme Makeover: Home Edition*, the Simpsons couldn't keep up with the property tax on the $600,000 house and had to sell it less than three years later.

Although it now has different owners, the Extreme Makeover house can still be seen on the corner of Abercorn and 55th Streets. Even in a neighborhood full of gorgeous brick mansions, the doll house-like home is impossible to miss.

EXTREME MAKEOVER: HOME EDITION HOUSE

WHAT: The "star" of a reality TV series

WHERE: Corner of Abercorn and 55th Streets, Savannah, GA

COST: Free

PRO TIP: The house is easy to admire from the street, but the residents' privacy should be respected.

51

THE HEARTBROKEN GIRL

How true is the tragic tale of Corinne Elliott Lawton?

In the tourist industry, particularly one as robust as Savannah's, narratives sometimes evolve that are more entertaining than factual and seem to take on a life of their own through repeated tellings. That is certainly the case of Corinne Elliott Lawton and her sorrowful statue in Bonaventure Cemetery.

Corinne was the daughter of Confederate Brigadier-General Alexander R. Lawton. The popular legend is that 19-year-old Corinne had fallen in love with a man her family didn't approve of and was forced to marry someone wealthier and with better position in society. Corinne was so despondent about marrying a man she didn't love that she flung herself into a river and drowned. This story has many variations, each more tragic (and melodramatic) than the next. In one version, Corinne kills herself on her wedding day. In another, she rides her horse into the Savannah River. Yet another has Corrine drown within sight of where she is currently buried.

Corinne's grave in Bonaventure is quite arresting, with a beautiful, lifelike statue by famed Sicilian sculptor Benedetto Civiletti. The statue depicts Corinne sitting at the foot of a cross with her dress falling from her shoulder and a crown of flowers dropped from her hand. Looking at her sad, resigned expression, it is easy to see

Artist Benedetto Civiletti used photographs of Corinne to create a realistic likeness.

The striking grave of Corrine Elliott Lawton's father stands behind her own.

CORINNE ELLIOTT LAWTON

WHAT: A beautiful monument to a life cut short

WHERE: Bonaventure Cemetery, 330 Bonaventure Road, Thunderbolt, GA 31404

COST: Free

NOTEWORTHY: The dramatic details of Corinne being engaged before her death is true, but unlike some of the stories, she wanted to get married.

how imaginations can run wild when speculating about her story. Her father's own impressive monument in the next plot over, with a statue of Jesus Christ smiling in her direction, has added fuel to the legend by suggesting that Corinne is rejecting her family by turning away from Jesus and her father.

Of course, the truth is not as dramatic, but it is just as tragic. According to the diary of Corinne's mother, she actually died at home from an illness (quite possibly yellow fever since the epidemic was just ending at the time of her death in 1877 at the age of thirty-one). Corinne's mother and father loved her very much and created a touching monument to their heartbreaking loss. Sometimes the truth is all you need.

52

THE ATOM SMASHERS

Which area high school has one of the most unusual mascots in the nation?

Vikings and Tigers and Bulldogs, oh my! These are just a few of the most commonly used mascot names used by high schools around the country. According to *USA Today*, Eagles takes the top spot with twenty-four schools using the name. It can't be that difficult to come up with an original mascot to represent the spirit of your school, can it? Sol C. Johnson High School in Savannah has the distinction of having one of the most interesting mascots in the nation, one that is as brainy as it is brawny: The Atom Smasher.

Opened in 1959, Sol C. Johnson High School was originally Powell Laboratory School, which ran under the direction of Savannah State University. Powell taught grades one through twelve, but when it became a high school, it was renamed after Solomon Charles Johnson, a philanthropist, educator, and founder of the *Savannah Tribune*, the nation's oldest newspaper printed primarily for the black community.

In 1961, the senior class designed and presented the school's coat of arms. A large letter "J" was surrounded by various symbolic objects loaded with meaning, including a gavel representing leadership, a quill for academic achievement, a trophy for athleticism, and a

THE ATOM SMASHERS SCULPTURE

WHAT: An unusual monument for an unusual team

WHERE: 3012 Sunset Blvd., Savannah, GA

COST: Free

NOTEWORTHY: Johnson High School's gym is called the "Reaction Chamber."

The sculpture has a charming, low-budget quality, but it still drives home the point.

laurel for honor. Surrounding the "J" was an atom, with the atom being a "symbol of unlimited potential energy." Thus, the Atom Smashers were born.

In 1962, a bronze sculpture was placed in front of the school to represent the Atom Smasher. It features a muscular arm wielding a gavel and a hand holding a spike, waiting for a powerful blow to drive it into a large atom. It's arguably more intimidating and thought provoking than an ordinary animal mascot. The Atom Smasher was named one of the five most unique mascots in the country by one poll.

The Atom Smashers turned up as a question on *Jeopardy*!

53 TOMOCHICHI'S BOULDER

Why is there a boulder in Wright Square?

Tomochichi, chief of the Yamacraw Indians, was integral to the founding of Georgia and Savannah. Without Tomochichi's strong leadership and artful mediation between Lower Creek chieftains and English settlers, General James Oglethorpe may never have successfully established the Georgia colony. When Tomochichi died in 1739, he wanted to be buried in Savannah, the city he helped create. To honor him, Oglethorpe, acting as a pallbearer, had Tomochichi buried in the center of Wright Square under a pyramid of stones.

In 1883, the City Fathers of Savannah wanted to erect a monument to William Washington Gordon, builder of Georgia's first railroad. By this time, Tomochichi's pyramid of stones was no longer in the square—just a dirt mound in its place. In fact, the stones had been missing since as early as the 1830s, likely removed intentionally when relations with Native Americans soured. If that is true, then what happened next shouldn't come as a surprise. The city plowed over Tomochichi's grave and plopped a towering monument to William Gordon on top.

Willam Washington Gordon's daughter-in-law, Nellie Gordon, felt so awful about the desecration of Tomochichi's grave, a man who had been so important to Savannah, that she and her cohorts in the Colonial Dames

---

Tomochichi's remains still lie under the Gordon monument.

128

The bronze tablet encircled with Cherokee roses and arrowheads says "In memory of Tomochichi – the Mico of the Yamacraws – the companion of Oglethorpe – and the friend and ally of the Colony of Georgia."

TOMOCHICHI MONUMENT

WHAT: A big boulder for a city founder

WHERE: The southeast corner of Wright Square, Savannah, GA

COST: Free

PRO TIP: A local legend says that if you walk around the boulder three times you'll hear Tomochichi say . . . nothing.

of America wrote to the Stone Mountain Company in Atlanta to request a suitable piece of granite for a monument. Stone Mountain offered a boulder free of charge, but Nellie wanted the donation to be from the Dames. According to the Colonial Dames' website, Stone Mountain sent a bill for $1.00 "payable on judgment day." Nellie paid the dollar with the reply, "The other ladies would be too busy attending to their own duties on that momentous day." The boulder monument to Tomochichi was placed in the southeast corner of Wright Square and dedicated on April 21, 1899. Let's see somebody try to move this one.

54 OINKS IN OSSABAW

Does an island in Georgia have its own breed of pig?

Ossabaw Island lies just twenty miles south of downtown Savannah, but if you want to visit, you're going to need a boat—and permission. One of the largest barrier islands in Georgia, Ossabaw is a paradise renowned for its natural beauty, with pristine, white sand beaches, wooded areas with oak-lined paths, and freshwater ponds that lure lots of wildlife.

Throughout the 1960s and 1970s, Ossabaw Island was run by the Ossabaw Foundation, founded by Sandy West and Clifford B. West. Through their Ossabaw Island Project, they made the island a creative retreat for artists and scientists. Writers, including Ralph Ellison and Margaret Atwood, spent time on the isolated island to work in peace. Even after the project ended in 1978 and the State of Georgia took over the island as a Heritage Preserve, the island continues to be used by authors for an annual writer's retreat.

Visitors need to apply for a trip to Ossabaw Island. They can come for a day trip to the beach, for a specially arranged two-night stay, or for organized hunting trips. The hunting trips are particularly important for the ecosystem of the island because of one of its most interesting but destructive residents: the Ossabaw hog.

Composers Aaron Copeland and Samuel Barber spent time at Ossabaw Island to work on music.

This hairy pig may be cute, but it can cause a lot of trouble in the island's ecosystem. (Photo by Justin Davis.)

OSSABAW ISLAND HOG

WHAT: A native feral pig

WHERE: Ossabaw Island, GA

COST: Depends on what you want to do on the island

NOTEWORTHY: Ossabaw hogs are now bred on the mainland for research (and artisanal pork), so if the pesky ones on the island have to be permanently removed (which is highly recommended by environmentalists), we won't lose one of Georgia's special little porkers.

The Ossabaw hog is a feral pig unique to the island. They are descended from pigs brought over in the sixteenth century by Spanish explorers and have been a bane to other creatures on the island ever since. The small, hearty hogs breed like crazy and are omnivorous, so they will eat anything and everything, including reptiles, roots, and furry animals. Their most detrimental impact on the ecology is eating the eggs of endangered species, such as loggerhead turtles and snowy plovers. Keeping the hogs in check is a full-time job, and there is a staff on the island to control the population with rifles.

55

FROM OGEECHEE TO SAVANNAH

Where can you explore one of the South's historic canals?

Before planes, trains, and automobiles . . . (and drones?) . . . the options for transporting large amounts of goods were pretty limited. Horses and carts are slow, and rivers only go where *they* want to go. Another less obvious but effective option was to dig your way there. That is what Georgia did when it chartered the Savannah-Ogeechee Canal in 1824. Between 1826 and 1830, African and Irish laborers dug a 16.5-mile canal connecting the Savannah River and the Ogeechee River (with six locks in-between), and for a while it was a boon for business in southern Georgia.

The first few years of the canal were a bit of a mess, as rotting wooden locks and constant erosion of the embankment eventually forced the parent company into bankruptcy. The new company improved the locks and widened the canal, and consequently it was successful for the next twenty years. Such goods as rice, cotton, bricks, and peaches from plantations were moved along the canal to markets.

SAVANNAH-OGEECHEE CANAL MUSEUM & NATURE CENTER

WHAT: A well-preserved example of nineteenth century transportation

WHERE: 681 Fort Argyle Road, Savannah, GA 31419

COST: $2

PRO TIP: The nature center has many local animals, including the state reptile—the gopher tortoise—and the state bird—the brown thrasher.

It may not be a highway, but this narrow waterway was briefly a vital part of Savannah's economy.

The canal was particularly important for moving lumber from the large sawmill located at the basin.

Use of the canal slowed down during the Civil War. Then when yellow fever hit the region, everyone blamed the canal for the severity of the outbreak, hurting business even more. By 1890, the canal shut down, replaced by railroads as the preferred mode of transport. Today, part of the canal is home to the Savannah-Ogeechee Canal Museum and Nature Center, where visitors can learn about the history of the canal and walk along several miles of trails that run through the 184 acres of swamp.

Slaves (later freemen) led mules up and down the canal as they towed barges.

56

THE "SEARS" HOUSE

Are those windows on right?

One of the most persistent, impossible-to-kill stories told to tourists when they come to Savannah is that of the house with the upside-down windows. It's unclear when and how this myth took hold, but even after being thoroughly debunked, it perseveres as a popular piece of local lore.

Here is the story as it has been told for years. Back when the Sears-Roebuck catalog was the Amazon.com of its day, shoppers could purchase nearly anything through mail order, including a kit house that you built yourself. The materials arrived by railcar, and the purchaser would assemble their friends and family to help assemble the house. It wasn't exactly "Tab A into Slot B," as the homes included modern amenities, such as central heating and indoor plumbing. Between 1908 and 1940, Sears sold an estimated 70,000 homes in North America, but when the kits were discontinued, sales records were destroyed, so identifying these homes today takes serious detective work.

The cute, peach-colored house with green shutters located on Habersham Street is supposedly one of these famed kit homes. The decorative touches on the bottom of the windows and what look like the windowsills on top, give the impression that somebody read the instructions

---

The windows look that way because they were designed to open from the top to let out the heat and keep things cool.

Once you get over the initial oddity of the windows, the house is actually quite attractive and worthy of attention on its own merits.

THE "SEARS" HOUSE

WHAT: A real estate rumor that won't die

WHERE: 32 habersham Street, Savannah, GA 31401

COST: Free

NOTEWORTHY: The house might not have been ordered from a catalog, but the fountain in Forsyth Park was.

wrong and installed the windows upside down. (They probably ended up with some leftover screws they didn't know what to do with too.) None of this is true, of course. As indicated by signs hung outside by the home's exasperated owners, the house is actually an "1889 Victorian Craftsman," and the windows are meant to look that way.

It may not truly be a kit home, and the windows aren't hilariously screwed up as originally believed, but the story, and its continual telling, makes the "Sears" house a worthy architectural attraction.

57

WALKING "BAWK"WARDS

Where did one of America's greatest writers teach a chicken to walk backwards?

Flannery O'Connor is one of the South's most beloved authors. The deeply sardonic writer, whose work is characterized as Southern gothic, penned the novels *Wise Blood* and *The Violent Bear It Away* as well as the short story collections *A Good Man Is Hard to Find* and *Everything That Rises Must Converge*. During her career, O'Connor won the O. Henry Award for Best Short Story three times and was posthumously awarded the National Book Award for *The Complete Stories*.

Flannery O'Connor's Historic Childhood Home in Savannah, where she lived from her birth in 1925 until 1938, is a modest house on Lafayette Square. With a view of St. John's Cathedral across the square, it's no wonder O'Connor had an intensely complex interest in Catholicism. The home now operates as a museum devoted to her life. Visitors can see O'Connor's room and some of her childhood belongings, learn about what life was like during the Great Depression, or catch one of the many literary events that are regularly hosted there.

There is more to O'Connor's legacy, though, than her literary achievements. Throughout her life, O'Connor's passion was raising chickens (and later peacocks), and she kept several in the garden of her Savannah home. One particular chicken was so remarkable that in 1932

Local writers and artists hold
a quirky annual parade at
O'Connor's home on her birthday.

Left, *With its history, library, and events, like the Ursrey Memorial Lecture, The Flannery O'Connor Childhood Home is an essential literary landmark.* Above, *The garden where O'Connor trained her renowned chicken.*

Pathé News sent a crew from New York to report on it. Later in life, O'Connor recalled the event with her typical sarcastic wit. "When I was six, I had a chicken that walked backward and was in the Pathé News," O'Connor said. "I was in it, too, with the chicken. I was just there to assist the chicken, but it was the high point of my life. Everything since has been an anticlimax."

Sure enough, you can still view the old news reel on YouTube of "Young Mary O'Connor" setting her chicken on the ground and making it walk backwards as a narrator cracks silly jokes about it. If you visit Flannery O'Connor's Childhood Home, be sure to walk through the garden where O'Connor's greatest accomplishment occurred.

FLANNERY O'CONNOR CHILDHOOD HOME

WHAT: The site where a young Flannery O'Connor did "stupid pet tricks"

WHERE: 207 East Charlton Street, Savannah, GA 31401

COST: $8 adults, $6 students/ military

PRO TIP: The home also contains the Bruckheimer Library, a collection of rare books.

58

BLOOD SUCKERS MUSEUM

Where can you see the world's largest collection of ticks?

Sandflies are pesky little biters, and mosquitoes can make the outdoors absolutely miserable, but no blood-sucking parasite in the South is as troublesome or tenacious as a tick. The little mites latch onto your warmest, hard-to-reach places and sip on you for days before you realize they're even there, by which time you have to pull the stubborn bugs out with tweezers (don't leave the head). Then there is the possibility of contracting Lyme disease or, God forbid, an allergy to red meat (from a Lone Star tick).

Most people would rather avoid ticks altogether, but for those who would like to learn more about them, Georgia Southern University in Statesboro houses the largest collection of ticks in the world. The U.S. National Tick Collection belongs to the Smithsonian's National Museum of Natural History but has been kept at GSU since 1990. The collection contains more than one million specimens (yikes!) from nearly 860 known species from every continent.

THE U.S. NATIONAL TICK COLLECTION

WHAT: Too many blood sucking parasites under one roof

WHERE: Georgia Southern University in the Math/Physics building, 1332 Southern Drive, Statesboro, GA 30458

COST: Free

PRO TIP: Visits to the USNTC are by appointment only, but a permanent exhibit just outside the collection is free to look at during normal building hours.

Above, *The exhibit's various displays will teach you more than you ever thought you wanted to learn about ticks.* Right, *How would you like to have this engorged thing attached to you?*

The collection actually serves an important role for researchers and public health officials studying the many diseases spread by parasites. The whole notion of so many ticks in one place may sound like a nightmare, but all the ticks are freeze-dried, bottled, and coated so that they are easier to observe under a microscope, and you don't have to worry about walking out of there with one hiding in your navel.

Ticks can be found in almost every environment, even in Antarctica, where *Ixodes uriae* feeds off of colonies of penguins.

59

PITCHES AT PULASKI

Where was the first known photo of a baseball game taken?

Baseball has been played for several centuries in one form or another, but it took a war to solidify it as "America's pastime." Baseball evolved from cricket and rounders, which came to America from England. The early rules for modern baseball began to be codified in New York City in 1845 and were known as the Knickerbocker Code. During the Civil War, Union soldiers took this form of the game and spread it throughout the West and South. There was a lot of downtime during the war, so thousands of soldiers picked it up to pass the time. When the war ended, soldiers brought this improved version of baseball home to teach to others.

Savannah's Fort Pulaski didn't escape the baseball bug during the war. In fact, one of the earliest photos of a baseball game was taken at Fort Pulaski in 1863. In the photo, Company H of the 48th New York Regiment is posing for a picture, but in the background one can see the other soldiers playing baseball. Considering the origin of the regiment, it could be assumed that they brought the Knickerbocker style south with them. There were still some differences from the game as we know it today. The rules required the "hurler" to pitch the ball rather than throw it, meaning it had to be an underhand toss like a horseshoe. It wasn't until 1884 that players could add a little heat with an overhand pitch. Baseball gloves weren't in use yet, but then again they probably didn't need them since the balls were usually made of bits of wood wrapped

Top, *A casual game of baseball is being played behind the 48th Regiment posing in the foreground. (Credit to National Park Service.)* Bottom, *Although the grand expanse of lawn would still make a suitable spot for a pick-up game, there is no record of anyone ever knocking a homer over Fort Pulaski's walls.*

FORT PULASKI

WHAT: The site of the first photographic evidence that baseball exists

WHERE: US-80, Savannah, GA 31410

COST: $10

PRO TIP: For dog owners, Fort Pulaski has the only beach in the area that allows pets.

in rags. Batters were known as "strikers," ground balls were called "daisy cutters," and the player could be caught out by a fly ball or a single bounce.

It may only be a coincidence, but if you look at an aerial view of Fort Pulaski, you will notice that the structure is shaped exactly like home plate.

60

SHELL SHOCK

Where can to you see the world's largest boiled peanut?

If you're from anywhere outside the South and enjoy peanuts, you are probably most familiar with the roasted variety—dry, crunchy, and salty. Once you head South, though, you may be surprised (or horrified) by how peanuts are prepared here. Boiled peanuts, which have been a folk tradition since the nineteenth century, are the antithesis to roasted peanuts—they are wet, soft, and briny—but don't let my unappetizing description dissuade you from trying them. Boiled peanuts are actually delicious, incredibly popular, and can be purchased from countless roadside stands or country convenience stores across the region.

In 2013, in nearby Bluffton, the "World's Largest Boiled Peanut" was constructed to hype the annual Bluffton Boiled Peanut Festival, which celebrates South Carolina's official state snack. Built by Jared Jester, Clayton Colleran, and Hannah Parrish, the 22-foot-long peanut was constructed out of pine studs, plywood, chicken wire, insulation, and exterior paint. After the festival, the sculpture was left on display at Cahill's Market and Restaurant.

The "World's Largest Boiled Peanut" sustained some damage when it was the star of an episode of A&E's *Shipping Wars* in 2014. The show features shippers

---

The large legume took thirty days to complete and weighs 800 pounds!

It may not be the only large peanut attraction in the South, but it is certainly one of the most impressive.

THE WORLD'S LARGEST BOILED PEANUT

WHAT: A monument to the South's favorite snack

WHERE: Cahill's Market, 1055 May River Road, Bluffton, SC 29910

COST: Free

PRO TIP: If you want to sound local, boiled peanuts are also called "goober peas."

competing to move unusual objects, and star Jessica Samko won the bid to move the peanut from roadside attraction South of the Border back to its home in Bluffton. Unfortunately, when loading the massive peanut on her flatbed truck, it kept rolling and fell off the other side, sustaining a large crack down the middle and some scrapes and gouges. Costar Marc Springer quipped upon delivery, "She already shelled it at the pickup." Samko paid $150 to repair the damage, and the peanut looks as shell-tastic as ever sitting outside of Cahill's Market.

61 DASHING THROUGH THE SNOW?

Was "Jingle Bells" really written in Savannah?

Thanks to the tourist industry, horses and carriages still clomp along the streets of Savannah as they have for centuries but one-horse open sleighs? Savannah has definitely never had those since it almost never snows here. Because of this lack of wintry weather, it may come as a surprise that one of the most iconic songs about enjoying the snow was written in Savannah.

James Lord Pierpont published "One Horse Open Sleigh," more commonly known as "Jingle Bells," on September 16, 1857, in Savannah. The full lyrics were once considered bawdy, and it was used as a drinking song. After all, the idea of a man and a woman taking an unchaperoned ride into the woods was improper. It had long been purported that Pierpont wrote the song in Medford, Massachusetts, while visiting a girlfriend. A plaque in Medford states the claim that Pierpont wrote "Jingle Bells" in 1850 in what was then Simpson's Tavern "in the presence of Mrs. Otis Waterman," and that it was inspired by the Salem Street sleigh races.

By the time Pierpont published the song, he was the organist and music

JINGLE BELLS

WHAT: A snowy Christmas classic written in Savannah

WHERE: Unitarian Universalist Church, 311 East Harris Street, Savannah, GA 31401

COST: Free

PRO TIP: To commemorate this interpretation of music history, a plaque was placed in Oglethorpe Square across from the Unitarian Church.

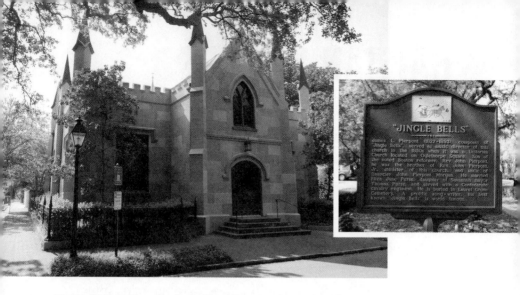

The Unitarian Church where Pierpont served as music director was located on Oglethorpe Square when he lived in Savannah.

director of the Unitarian Church in Savannah, where his brother, Rev. John Pierpont, Jr., was minister. Georgia historians disagree with Medford's claim to the song and believe Pierpont wrote "Jingle Bells" in Savannah when he was feeling nostalgic for New England. The truth is still up for debate, but the documented evidence leans in Savannah's favor. As a side note, although he was the son of the Boston abolitionist Rev. John Pierpont, James Pierpont was an active member of the Confederacy and wrote martial songs, such as "Strike for the South" and "We Conquer or Die." Not exactly singalong hits.

The song was originally written for Thanksgiving, but over the years it became associated with Christmas and the holiday season.

62

HAITIAN HEROES

Who were the foreign black soldiers that fought for American Independence?

The Siege of Savannah is considered one of the bloodiest battles of the Revolutionary War. The British had captured Savannah, so a year later, from September 16 to October 18, 1779, a Franco-American coalition attempted a siege to retake the city. The Americans were joined by the Chasseurs-Volontaires de Saint-Domingue, an all-black regiment from what is now Haiti. The Chasseurs-Volontaires were all volunteer soldiers, recruited from free men of color, and enlisted as part of a contingent of French troops sent to the South to assist the Americans. They were not only the largest black regiment to serve in the War of Independence, but with 545 soldiers, it was also the largest military unit to serve in the Siege of Savannah.

The British ended up winning that battle and held onto Savannah until 1782. When the war was over, some of the Chasseurs-Volontaires, battle-hardened and enlightened about the tyranny of colonization, returned home and helped lead the slave insurrections beginning in 1791 that led to the overthrow of the French, the end of slavery, and the formation of the first black government in the Western Hemisphere. Unfortunately, after fighting for America's independence, America, still a slaveholding nation, didn't return the favor and sided with the French during Haiti's own battle for freedom.

Thousands of soldiers of color, including the Chasseurs-Volontaires, fought in the Revolutionary War, but

---

The Chasseurs had the role of digging fortifications for the siege but ultimately fought in the front lines.

Above, *It has taken several centuries for the efforts of soldiers of color during the American Revolution to finally be recognized.* Right, *This little drummer boy grew up to become the King of Haiti.*

very few have ever been commemorated, and their efforts have been largely forgotten. To correct this exclusion from history, a monument to the Haitians who fought for America was erected in Franklin Square in 2007 (and completed in 2009). The statue, supported by the Miami-based Haitian-American Historical Society and sculpted by artist James Mastin, depicts six life-sized Chasseurs-Volontaires soldiers, all nameless except for one. The little drummer boy at the front of the group represents Henri Christophe, who allegedly fought in the Siege of Savannah as a teen before growing up to become the King of Haiti.

HAITIAN MONUMENT

WHAT: A tribute to Haiti's contribution to the American Revolution

WHERE: Franklin Square, Savannah, GA 31401

COST: Free

NOTEWORTHY: The monument was developed in two stages, with four figures erected in 2007 and then two more in 2009.

63

PUMP AND PET

Which I-16 gas station is also a petting zoo?

Interstate-16 is widely considered one of the most boring stretches of road in Georgia (if not the entire Southeast). The 166.8-mile highway connecting Macon and Savannah is an absolute slog for drivers, and for those with children it can be even worse. With very little of interest to see for hours other than endless rows of pine trees, any respite from the tedium is welcome. Fortunately, in Metter at Highway 57, Exit 98, there is a little oasis of diversion at the Wiregrass Junction Chevron station. When you are done topping off your tank and purchasing beef jerky, you and your family can stretch your legs at Mosley's World Famous Animal Exit Farm.

When owner Holt Mosley and his brother, Stan, built the Wiregrass Junction convenience store in 1996, they added a petting zoo to attract families who were looking to take a break from the road. The farm actually offers quite a lot to see, as the menagerie of animals has grown over the last twenty years. Like any typical petting zoo, there are goats, donkeys, llamas, and a tortoise in a petting area, but there is also an exotic bird barn with peacocks and parrots, and a pasture ride where you can see the more impressive animals on display from a van. The trail features camels, long-haired pigs, emus, a zebra,

Some animal residents include a type of African cow called a Watusi and a miniature Brahma bull named Zebu.

Top, *Mosley is slowly changing the name of his safari to "Wild Georgia Animal Park," and merchandise currently reflects both names.* Bottom, *There are not too many places where you can see zebras and camels in the same enclosure.*

MOSLEY'S WORLD FAMOUS ANIMAL EXIT FARM

WHAT: A gas station/petting zoo to distract your bored children

WHERE: I-16 Exit 98, Metter, GA

COST: $2 for entry, $1 for feed, $10 for the full experience

PRO TIP: Many animals are here, so you may want to buy more than one bag of food.

bison, horses, a kangaroo, a water buffalo, antelope, and a monkey. Swimming in a large pond are swans, duck, and geese.

Mosley's farm is surprisingly fun, and you won't find another gas station like it. The sign on Mosley's promises that their farm offers "The Best Dollar Spent On I-16," and for thirty minutes of happy, uncomplaining children and relief from the road, they might be right.

64 THE DOWN-SOUTH SUBMARINE

Where can you learn the history of the kazoo?

If you can hum, then you can play the "most democratic" instrument in the world—the kazoo. The modest instrument is right up there with the recorder and the baby xylophone as the first instrument people learn to play. It takes only a moment to learn and no time to master. The humble kazoo has a silly, buzzy sound that made it popular in vaudeville, comedy, and jazz acts of old, and it continues to be a popular American musical invention. There is even a National Kazoo Day celebrated on January 28.

The kazoo has several different origin stories. The most commonly told story about the invention of the kazoo is that it was created in 1840 by a German clockmaker named Thaddeus Von Clegg for an African-American entertainer from Macon, Georgia, named Alabama Vest, who later called it the "Down-South Submarine" when he presented it at the 1852 Georgia State Fair. No documentation proves this story, however, so it's hard to know how much of it is true. A more verifiable story is that the American inventor Warren Herbert Frost named his instrument/toy "kazoo" when he patented it in 1883. The submarine-shaped kazoo we know today was later

Customers of Kazoobie Kazoos include Weezer and flautist Ian Anderson of Jethro Tull.

A re-creation of where clockmaker Thaddeus Von Clegg invented the kazoo.

KAZOO MUSEUM

WHAT: A large collection of little plastic hummers

WHERE: Kazoobie Kazoo Factory, 12 John Galt Road, Beaufort, SC 29906

COST: Free

PRO TIP: If you aren't convinced that kazoos are awesome, watch the "You on Kazoo" video on YouTube.

patented by George D. Smith of Buffalo, New York, in 1902, but it was the Original American Kazoo Company, which opened in 1916, that began to mass-produce it to make it a part of American musical culture.

Visitors to nearby Beaufort, South Carolina, can learn more about the history of the kazoo at the Kazoo Museum, located at the Kazoobie Kazoo Factory. The museum features more than 200 kazoos, making it one

Who knew there was so much to learn about the kazoo?

of the largest kazoo collections in the world. Some of the unique pieces include kazoos shaped like cartoon characters, an electric kazoo, a kazoo used in *The Partridge Family* television show, and several kazoos that are more than 100 years old. Visitors can also visit the factory to see how kazoos are made and then construct their own from fourteen different body colors and custom-made resonators. Sometimes, the silliest attractions are the best, so give the Kazoo Museum a visit and see what all the "buzz" is about.

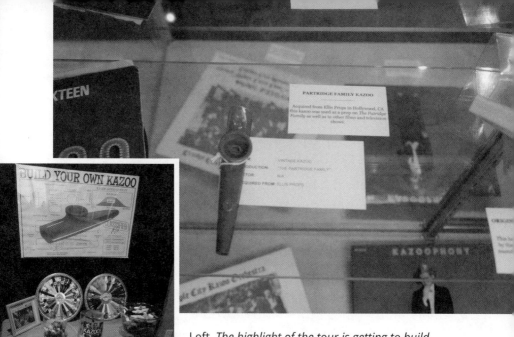

Left, *The highlight of the tour is getting to build your own colorful, custom kazoo.* Above, *This kazoo used in the Partridge Family is an example of the many instruments on display.*

65 COCKTAILS AND POETRY

Where can you have martinis with a dead poet?

There is a moment early on in John Berendt's book *Midnight in the Garden of Good and Evil* where Berendt enjoys a martini at Conrad Aiken's grave with a Savannah society lady. It's a moment that highlights one of Savannah's more obscure but delightful traditions for lovers of literature.

Conrad Aiken is an American poet and writer who was born in Savannah on August 5, 1889. When Aiken was eleven years old, he witnessed the murder-suicide of his mother and father and moved to Cape Cod, Massachusetts, to be raised by relatives. After graduating from Harvard (where he was a classmate of T.S.Eliot), Aiken went on to write fifty novels, short stories, and essays, but he was most renowned for his poetry. Throughout his career, Aiken earned a Pulitzer Prize, a National Book Award, and a National Medal of Literature. He was also appointed Georgia's Poet Laureate in 1973 by then Governor Jimmy Carter.

In 1962, Aiken moved back to Savannah and into the house right next door to his childhood home where his parents were killed and lived there until his death on August 17, 1973. Aiken and

CONRAD AIKEN'S GRAVE

WHAT: A cemetery bench devoted to books and booze

WHERE: Bonaventure Cemetery, 330 Bonaventure Road, Thunderbolt, GA 31404

COST: Free

PRO TIP: Some visitors to Aiken's grave go so far as to drink out of red votive candleholders—a tradition Aiken supposedly picked up from Ernest Hemingway and his friends during their moveable feast.

Left, *Conrad Aiken is buried next to his parents where he spent many evenings during his lifetime.* Right, *Aiken's grave offers a nice place to sit in the cemetery.*

his third wife, Mary, are buried in Bonaventure Cemetery right next to his parents' plot. Instead of a gravestone, their marker is a granite bench. During their lifetime, Conrad and Mary used to visit his parents' grave and enjoy martinis while gazing in contemplation at the Wilmington River. Local legend says that Aiken wanted a bench on his grave so that poetry lovers could sit there and enjoy a few drinks in the cemetery.

Today, many locals and visitors carry on the tradition by bringing a thermos of martini to Conrad Aiken's grave.

Aiken's bench bears the inscriptions "Cosmos Mariner-Destination Unknown" and "Give My Love to the World."

66 THE LITTLE DOOR TO NOWHERE

What is the little door at 145 Bull Street for?

Just inside the arched entryway of a bricked path that leads through the building at 145 Bull Street to the lane on the other side is an unusually small door set in the left wall. The door has been a curiosity for passersby for decades. Other than being about one-third scale, the diminutive door looks like an ordinary door—dark green with four panels, a doorknob, a deadbolt, and a mail slot. The most unusual aspect is not the size of the door but that it apparently doesn't lead anywhere, as the wall on the other side of where the doorway would seemingly lead is bare.

The door poses a lot of questions, many of which lead the imagination down a rabbit hole. Why is it locked? Who has the key? What happens if you knock on it? Will somebody answer? What happens if you lift the mail slot and peer inside? Will something look back at you? Who put this door here? Do leprechauns board here during St. Patrick's Day? If you open it, will it take you to Narnia? Or down a literal rabbit hole?

Does anyone else see this strange door?

As it turns out, the answers to these questions are not quite so magical. According to the owner of the hair

---

The door makes for a fun photo opportunity for those who want to look taller.

Who installed this curious door and why?

A LITTLE DOOR

WHAT: A mysterious door to nowhere

WHERE: 145 Bull Street, Savannah, GA 31401

COST: Free

PRO TIP: You might be surprised by what looks back at you if you look in the mail slot.

salon next door, the little door is actually a mailbox of sorts. Apparently, mail really is dropped into the little mail slot, and those residents with the key can retrieve it. It's unclear when the mailbox was installed or why it looks like a regular (albeit small) door, but it is a cute and unusual attraction that catches the attention of eagle-eyed people who notice it.

67 A WORLD DIVIDED

What is the Cracked Earth Monument?

The Savannah Gas Company globe off DeRenne Avenue is not the only large representation of the earth in Savannah. "A World Apart" is a World War II Monument located on the River Street waterfront that honors the many Chatham County citizens who gave their lives in the European and Pacific theaters. The sculpture, more commonly known as the Cracked Earth Monument, took almost ten years to plan and fund before it was dedicated in 2010.

The massive bronze and copper globe is split in two to symbolize the division of the world into two theaters of war. Visitors can walk between the halves and read the names of 527 Chatham County service people who were killed in the war inscribed on the inner walls. Outside the globe is a Purple Heart and a WWII Victory Medal. The sculpture was designed by architect Eric Meyerhoff and built by Ken Brandell of Key Largo, Florida.

The Cracked Earth Monument faced its share of controversy during the planning stages. It was originally supposed to be erected in the middle of Oglethorpe Square, but residents complained that, at a planned 25-foot width and 19-foot height, the monument was

---

The original design featured eight life-size bronze figures by artist Susan Chisholm that represented members of the Army, Navy, Army Air Corps, Marines, Coast Guard, Merchant Marines, women in the armed forces, and nurses.

It may have been too big for the squares, but the Cracked Earth Monument is well suited for the Riverfront where it attracts visitors who want to honor those lost in World War II.

CRACKED EARTH MONUMENT

WHAT: A monument to a world divided by war

WHERE: River Street, Savannah, GA 31401

COST: Free

PRO TIP: The monument sits in front of the Bohemian Hotel.

going to be way too big and overwhelm the square (and draw attention away from other points of interest, such as the Historic Owens-Thomas House). The city wanted the design to be reduced by 25 percent, but the Veterans Council of Chatham County, who proposed the project, balked at the idea. Ultimately, some proposed life-sized bronze figures be dropped from the design, and the location was moved to River Street. The move was for the better, since River Street had more history tied to World War II with Liberty ships having been built in its shipyards.

Why is Driftwood Beach one of the South's most beautiful coastlines?

Depending on your point of view, Driftwood Beach is one of the most beautiful beaches in the Southeast or one of the creepiest. Up and down a stretch of beach on the northern end of Jekyll Island, scatterings of dead trees reach out of the sand like the gnarled, skeletal hands of long buried titans. The uncanny phenomena is the result of slow erosion caused by soft, barely lapping waves that gradually move the sand to the south end of the island. The oaks and pine trees eventually die and get uprooted but don't get pulled back into the ocean by the current. Instead, the trees bleach in the sun until the beach resembles an elephant boneyard.

Visitors love to wander through the labyrinth of tangled branches. The exposed root systems of fallen trees draw the eye into their jumble of shapes and textures. Some twisty trees are still standing and look absolutely striking against the minimal canvas of sea and sky behind them—especially at sunrise. Despite the desolate, otherworldly atmosphere that the dead trees convey, Driftwood Beach is actually a favorite spot for artists, photographers, and even weddings.

Driftwood Beach was once a maritime forest that was eaten slowly over time by the sea.

Like monuments in a cemetery, the dead, expressive trees of Driftwood beach can convey beauty as well as sadness.

DRIFTWOOD BEACH

WHAT: An eerie but picturesque natural phenomenon

WHERE: Jekyll Island

COST: Free

PRO TIP: Countless examples of beautiful photographs of Driftwood Beach can be seen online.

Driftwood Beach extends from the Clam Creek Picnic Area to the Villa by the Sea Resort. There are several access points along the way, including from Jekyll Island Campground or from North Beachview Drive.

69 THE TRIDENT OF TIME

What is the world's largest figurative sundial?

Hilton Island may be a popular golf vacation destination for us mere mortals, but even the Roman God of the Sea appreciates the area's breezy waterfront dining and fashionable shopping options. Okay, not really, but you can still see a striking representation of King Neptune towering godlike in front of Shelter Cove Harbour at Palmetto Dunes.

The 12-foot-tall bronze statue of King Neptune wielding his famed trident is the largest *figurative* sundial in the world. The bearded statue stands at the top of a 26-foot-diameter sundial with his trident thrust toward the ground—as though he were spearing the Kraken—acting as the gnomon that casts a shadow on the dial. Numbers arranged around the dial accurately indicate the month and hour of the day.

The King Neptune sundial was sculpted and installed by artist Wayne Edwards in 1983. It was cast in Princeton, New Jersey, and then shipped by truck (not sea?) to Hilton Head Island. In an act of scientific engineering, with a history that can be traced back to ancient Egyptian and Babylonian times, careful measurements were made to make sure that the one-ton statue was oriented to face true south by aligning his trident with the North Star and Ursa Major. The sundial

KING NEPTUNE SUNDIAL

WHAT: A godlike timepiece

WHERE: 13 Harbourside Lane, Hilton Head Island, SC 29928

COST: Free

PRO TIP: Neptune isn't the only sea dweller in Shelter Cove Harbour. A statue of a mermaid is by the nearby minipark.

Neptune is also the god of horses and is often depicted riding a horse-drawn chariot across the sea.

is fully functional, and although it doesn't tell the exact minute of the hour, you can still use it to make sure you don't miss your tee time.

King Neptune is big, but the tallest sundial in the world is the 73-foot-tall Samrat Yantra in Jaipur, India.

What famous Savannah landmark stood in for Africa in a popular television series?

Wormsloe Historic Site (also known as Wormsloe Plantation) on the Isle of Hope is widely considered one of the most beautiful historic landmarks in Savannah. The plantation was the home of Noble Jones, a carpenter who arrived in Georgia in 1733 with James Oglethorpe and the first settlers, and who is revered as one of Savannah's founding members. The ruins of Jones' fortified tabby house, built in 1745, is the oldest standing structure in Savannah. Visitors come to Wormsloe for its trails, historical tours, and costumed colonial interpretations, but the highlight of the plantation is the mile-long road that leads to the site from the entrance. With mossy oaks lined up on either side of the road, the branches create a picturesque, natural archway.

There is a common misconception that the "Run, Forrest, Run!" scene from the movie *Forrest Gump* was shot on this stretch of road, and it's an honest mistake to make. The actual film location for this scene was in Yemassee, South Carolina, and its tree-lined path does bear a striking resemblance to Wormsloe. *Forrest Gump* may not have been shot at Wormsloe, but another iconic production was filmed there.

When the producers of *Roots*, the Emmy Award–winning television miniseries from 1977 about the Atlantic slave trade, were scouting for locations for their series, they were mostly searching in Southern California. In

Roots remains one of the highest-rated U.S. programs in television history.

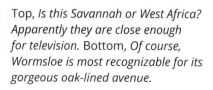

Top, *Is this Savannah or West Africa? Apparently they are close enough for television*. Bottom, *Of course, Wormsloe is most recognizable for its gorgeous oak-lined avenue.*

WORMSLOE STATE HISTORIC SITE

WHAT: Savannah's Africa

WHERE: 7601 Skidaway Road, Savannah, GA 31406

COST: $10 adults, $4.50 youth, $2 children under 6

PRO TIP: Wormsloe's "Colonial Faire and Muster" is a highlight of Georgia Day in February.

the book *Inside the Story of T.V.'s "Roots,"* producer Stan Margulies recounted that no place in California even remotely resembled West Africa, and there was not a big enough budget to actually film in Africa. Marguiles was terrified that if they tried to pass California off as Africa the show would be a "total disaster." Fortunately, after more scouting, *Roots* author Alex Haley visited Savannah, agreed that the salt flats at Wormsloe looked close enough to Gambia, and television history was made.

71 GRAVEFACE

Where can you find a wealth of oddities, including art by serial killers?

Ryan Graveface considers himself a hoarder and over the years has accumulated a monumental collection of vinyl records, bizarre taxidermy, VHS movies, horror memorabilia, and other oddities. Sure, he could have kept his treasure trove to himself, but instead he opened Graveface Records and Curiosities in the artsy Starland District of Savannah to share some of his valuable collection. With thousands of cool records to dig through, it would be enough to dub Graveface the best record store in Savannah, but there is so much more to it than that.

If you don't care for vinyl, the store is still a veritable must-see museum of the weird. The walls are adorned with creepy, old Halloween costumes (Ryan's favorite holiday, of course); horror movie posters, including wild, gory, hand-painted ones from Ghana; freakish taxidermy, such as two-headed skateboarding ducklings and squirrels throwing obscene gestures; and, most unsettlingly, artwork painted by an infamous serial killer. Displayed behind the glass counter is a portrait of "The Plainfield Ghoul" himself, Ed Gein, painted by the original creepy killer clown, John Wayne Gacy. Ryan began buying up serial killer art and memorabilia years ago and has since amassed a collection, including twenty paintings by Gacy, drawings by Charles Manson and Richard Ramirez, journals

Ryan Graveface also runs the Graveface Records record label and its sister label Terror Vision, which releases vinyl pressings of classic and cult horror movie sound tracks.

GRAVEFACE RECORDS & CURIOSITIES

WHAT: A mecca for music and macabre oddities

WHERE: 5 West 40th Street, Savannah, GA 31401

COST: Free

PRO TIP: Most of the items are priced to sell, but Ryan is open to offers for everything else.

Left, *Graveface's music selection is as eclectic as the crazy stuff on the walls.* Right, *This painting of a serial killer by another serial killer is just a taste of the strange collection of Graveface.*

and letters, and even shoes worn by John Lotter (the inspiration for the movie *Boys Don't Cry*), although he only displays most of it during special art exhibits and events.

In October 2019, Graveface Records will experience some exciting expansions. Ryan, a rabid movie fan, is turning the annex next door to his shop into an exact replica of the old video store that he frequented as a child and honed his gruesome obsessions. Then down on Savannah's famous Factor's Walk on River Street, Ryan is developing the Graveface Museum in a large, untouched nineteenth-century warehouse. The macabre museum will showcase his extensive true crime collection, weird UFO material (Ryan may have been abducted as a child), old circus décor and memorabilia, horror and Halloween material, and much more. Fans of everything strange and horrific should make sure to visit all of Graveface's locations.

Where can you purchase old maps for almost anywhere?

It really wasn't that long ago that we relied on maps instead of GPS to find our way in the world. Some experts believe that as convenient as GPS can be for finding our way around, looking at a printed map is better for connecting to and understanding one's surroundings. (Seriously, how many times have you plugged a location into a GPS and couldn't describe to anyone how you reached your destination when asked later?)

For John Duncan and his wife, Virginia (Ginger to her friends), cartography is king. The classically genteel Southern couple have run V & J Duncan's Antique Maps, Prints, and Books out of their ornate, three-story Second Baroque Townhouse on Monterey Square in Savannah's Historic District since 1983. The Duncans have amassed a collection of more than 4,000 maps, most from the eighteenth and nineteenth centuries, that attracts cartography enthusiasts from all over the world. There are old maps of Savannah, every U.S. state, and most other countries as well as celestial maps dating as far back as the seventeenth century.

The Duncans are particularly interested in maps with mistakes, some intentional and some due to laziness. For example, many mapmakers used to add trap (fake) streets to their maps to foil forgers. Some old maps of California depict it as an island, a mistake that other cartographers continued to depict because they couldn't

John Duncan acted as John Berendt's tour guide when he was writng *Midnight in the Garden of Good and Evil*.

Left, The Duncan's run their business out of the bottom floor of their stunning house. *Above,* Along with maps and prints, customers can also purchase a copy of John Duncan's latest book, The Showy Town of Savannah, *about architect William Jay.*

bother to look at updated engraving plates. Other maps feature anomalies, such as diminished-sized countries, thanks to political or racial biases. Each map in the shop is a piece of history as well as a piece of art, with many having decorative cartouches in the corners depicting palm trees, animals, exotic birds, American Indians, and unicorns. Many customers purchase the maps to hang on their walls, and the prices are surprisingly reasonable. The vast collection at V & J Duncan's also includes old engravings, mezzotints, lithographs, photographs, and rare, old, leatherbound books, as well as tens of thousands of portraits and prints featuring architecture, birds, fashion, and botanicals.

If you are trying to determine where you are or where you're going next, V & J Duncan's Antique Maps shop is a good place to begin.

V & J DUNCAN'S ANTIQUE MAPS, PRINTS, AND BOOKSTORE

WHAT: A cartographer's dream

WHERE: 12 East Taylor Street, Savannah, GA 31401

COST: Free to look

PRO TIP: Many of the maps can be viewed on their website, www.vjduncan.com.

73 THE SEAMEN'S BETHEL

Where do passing sailors stop to rest?

The common pop culture perception of sailors is a rowdy, hard-living bunch, but the truth is that they are just regular people working in a tough, lonely line of work. Tens of thousands of sailors from more than fifty countries have come through the port of Savannah every year for centuries. Spending months at sea, with no land in sight, away from homes and families, can be both physically and spiritually taxing for the seamen. Even today when foreign sailors come into port, they may have only half a day to run errands, contact family, and just savor the solid ground beneath their feet, and they may need help with transportation, medical issues, getting a meal, or finding Internet access to connect with home. Fortunately, the city has a place just for them that is surprisingly little known by regular citizens. In fact, most people pass this house on Washington Square every day and have no clue what it is really for or that it even still operates.

The Savannah Port Society was founded in 1843 by a group of churches looking for a way to contact and assist visiting seamen. While ministers spend time at the ports visiting sailors on the ships and administering to their religious needs, the International Seamen's House on Houston Street offers a hospitable refuge for weary travelers. The house is run by Evelyn Singleton,

A burial ground in Laurel Grove Cemetery specifically for seamen who die in Savannah was donated to the Society in 1860.

This humble house on Washington Square has offered respite to weary sailors since 1965.

INTERNATIONAL SEAMEN'S HOUSE

WHAT: A sanctuary for sailors

WHERE: 25 Houston Street, Savannah, GA 31401

COST: Free, but they are in need of donations to continue their work.

PRO TIP: They are also always looking for volunteers.

who seafarers affectionately call "Mom." Evelyn took over duties at the Seamen's House and chapel after her husband, Reverend Curtis Singleton, with whom she moved to Savannah in 1992 to manage the ministry, passed away. Evelyn lives upstairs and keeps the downstairs chapel and other rooms available for arriving seamen. Evelyn also drives around in a van, picking up foreign sailors and taking them to the house to eat, get some rest, or use the phone or Internet. She also takes them on shopping errands and even once helped a man pick up a wedding dress his fiancé had ordered from a dress shop in Savannah.

There are only a handful of ministers running the operation, but the Savannah Port Society and International Seamen's House continue the long tradition of warmly welcoming thousands of seafarers to Savannah and giving them a place to recharge before returning to the sea.

74 CHOO CHOO AT THE ROUNDHOUSE

Where can you see an antebellum train repair facility?

Steam, smoke, and ear-piercing whistles still emit from the Georgia State Railroad Museum, the largest and most intact antebellum train repair facility in the world. The complex was built in 1855 by the Central of Georgia Railroad, and of its original structures, thirteen remain, including the roundhouse and its functional turntable, which is still used to turn trains around to the delight of tourists and children.

The Central of Georgia Railroad was chartered in 1833 and for more than 100 years had an important role in Savannah's economy. In the 1920s, it was the largest employer in the city, but diesel engines eventually rendered the repair facility obsolete, and it shut down in 1963. Today, the roundhouse and facility are owned by the city of Savannah and operated by the Coastal Heritage Society.

The roundhouse still shelters antique trains and railcars, including some swanky, old executive cars that visitors can walk through. Five of the buildings are used for exhibits, including a print shop, a boiler house, coach and paint shops, a collection of antique machinery, and

---

A partial carpentry shop has been converted into the Savannah Children's Museum, a beautiful bricked enclosure that is worth a visit on its own.

The old diesel train emits a piercing whistle before giving visitors a ride on the turnaround and across the facilities.

THE GEORGIA STATE RAILROAD MUSEUM

WHAT: A playground for train enthusiasts

WHERE: 655 Louisville Road, Savannah, GA 31401

COST: $11 adults, $7 children

PRO TIP: The handcar rides are fun.

an H-O scale model train set that looks like downtown Savannah. Towering in the center of the complex is a 125-foot smokestack that has small tunnels lining the base . . . which are actually privies. Although, the smokestack and its privies are no longer in use, a child (i.e., the author's son) might occasionally slip away and use a privy for its originally intended purpose.

The museum keeps several examples of steam and diesel rolling stock, such as a Baldwin C-3 class 2-8-0 that was built in 1907, and there are several opportunities during the day to take a (short) ride on one of their trains. The Georgia State Railroad Museum is great for train buffs and children.

75 IT'S MARITIME IN SAVANNAH

Where can you learn about the *SS Savannah* and its historic journey?

Savannah has a plane museum, a train museum, and an automobile museum, but where would one find a ship museum? Naturally, in the historic home of William Scarbrough (1776–1838), one of the owners of the *SS Savannah*, the first steamship to cross the Atlantic. Scarbrough's Greek Revival house, which he called "the Castle," was built in 1819 by famed architect William Jay. Scarbrough's wealth was on the rise when he invested in the *SS Savannah*, but although it successfully made the trip across the ocean, it proved to be commercially unviable, and Scarbrough lost his shirt. He had only been in his new house for a few years before he went bankrupt and had to sell it and all of its furnishings.

In the 1870s, after passing through several owners, Scarbrough House became the first public school for African-American children. The West Broad Street School, as it was now known, ran until it was closed in 1962. The house remained unused other than for brief periods of renovation until 1995 when it housed the Ships of the Sea Maritime Museum.

The Ships of the Sea Maritime Museum has nine galleries of ship models, paintings, and artifacts. The

It took nearly thirty years for another American steamship to cross the Atlantic Ocean after the *SS Savannah*'s milestone.

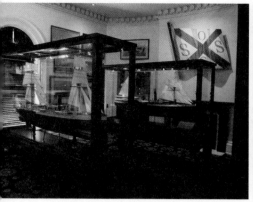

Left, *Dozens of immaculately detailed model ships are on display in the mansion's many rooms.* Right, *William Scarbrough's "Castle" is an architectural marvel that went through years of disuse before being restored to its former glory.*

SHIPS OF THE SEA MARITIME MUSEUM

WHAT: A museum dedicated to Savannah's greatest ships

WHERE: 41 Martin Luther King Blvd., Savannah, GA 31401

COST: $9 adults, $7 students

PRO TIP: You can learn more about their online exhibits at www.shipsofthesea.org/online-exhibits.

models, housed in glass display cases, are stunningly detailed re-creations of famous ships from Savannah's history and maritime history in general. There is, of course, a model of the *SS Savannah* as well as the *Anne*, the ship that brought Georgia's first colonists in 1733, and the *Wanderer*, a slippery, fast pleasure yacht that was repurposed to sneak slaves into the United States long after the importation of slaves was outlawed . . . and no model ship collection would be complete without the *Titanic*.

The Ships of the Sea Maritime Museum is also known for having the largest private gardens in the historic district. The nineteenth century–style parlor garden and award-winning North Garden are popular for weddings and concerts. After years of neglect, the Scarbrough House has become the center of Savannah's nautical past.

HOME OF THE BANANAS

What minor league stadium hosted some of baseball's greatest legends?

New York has the Yankees. Atlanta has the Braves. Savannah has the . . . Bananas? The Savannah Bananas, the city's beloved collegiate Coastal Plains League team, are just the latest in a long line of baseball teams that have made a home in historic Grayson Stadium. Over the decades, Grayson Stadium has been the home field for the minor league affiliates of the Cleveland Indians, Kansas City Athletics, Cincinnati Reds, Pittsburgh Pirates, Chicago White Sox, Washington Senators, and Atlanta Braves. Originally called Municipal Stadium when it opened in 1926, Grayson Stadium is the oldest continuously running minor league ballpark in America and still retains a lot of its old-fashioned charm (like a hand-turned scoreboard).

Many of the greatest ballplayers of all time have hit Grayson Stadium's field. In 1927, Lou Gehrig played an exhibition game there. In 1935, Babe Ruth visited the field to play the local Georgia Teachers College. In 1959, Mickey Mantle played at Grayson Stadium when the Yankees and Reds played an exhibition game.

In 1951, Jackie Robinson became the first black player to break the color barrier at Grayson Stadium when the Dodgers played the Phillies in an exhibition game. Two years after this milestone the Savannah Indians, along with the rest of the Southern Atlantic League—or Sally League—finally integrated.

GRAYSON STADIUM

WHAT: A minor league stadium for major league talent

WHERE: 1401 East Victory Drive, Savannah, GA 31404

COST: Tickets vary

PRO TIP: Tickets to Bananas games are hard to come by, so order early.

Left, *The Bananas have broken attendance records thanks to excellent promotion and a fun, family-oriented atmosphere at every game. The owner is at every game wearing a yellow suit and top hat, while his wife entertains the fans as the Banana's mascot.* Right, *Although it didn't count towards his stats, home run record holder Hank Aaron knocked one out of this park, as well.*

The most unusual celebrity to visit Grayson Stadium was comedian Sasha Baron Cohen's Borat in an episode from the first season of *Da Ali G Show*. Borat, on a mission to learn about America's pastime, attended a Savannah Sand Gnats game, where he hilariously treated the unsuspecting crowd to his overly long rendition of the Kasakhstan national anthem and then visited the Sand Gnat players in the locker room shower after the game. To Savannah's credit, the team and fans were incredibly hospitable and friendly to Borat.

Savannah may have lost their minor league team a few years ago when the Sand Gnats moved away, but the Savannah Bananas have taken up the baseball mantle in grand fashion, winning the Coastal Plains League championship in its inaugural season and regularly selling out tickets, a feat rarely achieved by Savannah's previous minor league teams.

Such legends as Ty Cobb, Hank Aaron, Stan Musial, and Ted Williams have played at Grayson Stadium.

77 REVOLUTIONARY BAR

Where did Georgians meet regularly to sow a revolution and create a government?

When you and your compatriots get riled up about something, what better place is there to meet up and vent about it than at your local watering hole. That is what Georgia colonists did when they convened at Tondee's Tavern in Savannah on August 10, 1774, to complain about British rule. The Boston Tea Party had occurred in Massachusetts just nine months earlier, sparking what would soon become the American Revolution. With colonists in an uproar about British policy and a Continental Congress called for in Virginia, Georgia's Royal Governor James Wright issued an order forbidding gatherings from meeting and speaking out against Great Britain. That didn't stop thirty Georgia representatives, calling themselves the Sons of Liberty, from meeting at Tondee's Tavern to draft resolutions condemning the Intolerable Acts and unfair taxes. Peter Tondee himself stood at the door with a list like a bouncer to make sure no uninvited guests got in.

On June 5, 1775, the rebellious Sons of Liberty met at Tondee's again to celebrate the king's birthday. With war breaking out, the pumped-up patriots erected a liberty pole, drank thirty toasts with accompanying cannon fire, and paraded through the streets with rifles and

In 2013, a restaurant opened on Bay Street bearing the name Tondee's Tavern to keep the legend alive. As far as anyone knows, no revolutions have been hatched in the new Tondee's Tavern . . . yet.

This spot on the corner of Whitaker Street was where the first Georgia government was shaped.

bayonets. In July, Georgia's Second Provincial Congress met at Tondee's, where they elected representatives for the Continental Congress and created the first government of Georgia. Peter Tondee died in October 1775, but his wife, Lucy, continued to run Tondee's Tavern, where it remained the center of Georgia's Provincial Congress until the British captured Savannah in 1778. After the British left in 1782, the Congress continued to use Tondee's Tavern as the seat of government until they moved to Augusta in 1785.

Unfortunately, Tondee's Tavern burned down in the Great Savannah Fire of 1796, but in 1899 the Georgia Society of Colonial Dames of America put a plaque on the building at the corner of Whitaker and Broughton Streets to mark the site where Georgia's government was born.

78 SPHERE IN THE SQUARE

Why does a Troup Square sculpture have more to do with astrology than history?

Savannah has no lack of monuments and sculptures strewn about the city. Most of the structures represent Savannah's long, rich history: for example, Georgia's founding fathers, American Revolutionary War heroes, religious leaders, industry tycoons, the African-American experience. One of the city's most unusual and striking sculptures, however, has nothing to do with history (Savannah's anyway).

The Armillary Sphere in the center of Troup Square was the source of some controversy when it was constructed and erected in the early 1970s, since at that point it was the most modern sculpture in the city. "Modern" is a bit of a misnomer considering that the armillary was invented by the ancient Greeks and Chinese thousands of years ago. An armillary is a device used to track heavenly movements with a sphere (the earth or the sun) in the center and a series of metal rings around it to represent lines of celestial longitude and latitude, and other paths. The armillary was rendered obsolete with the invention of the telescope, but it remains a fascinating and beautiful art object.

Troup Square's Armillary Sphere is a large bronze-alloy structure resting on six bronze turtles. There are gold zodiac signs around the rings and a lance passing through the center of the sphere. Although it probably won't be of much use for astrology or astronomy, the

The armillery was damaged in 2004 when it was hit by a drunk driver, but it has since been repaired.

Above, *It's the Armillary Sphere's ahistorical qualities that make it one of the most unique sculptures in Savannah.* Inset, *The armillary rests on the backs of several bronze turtles, but it is unclear what turtles have to do with the cosmos.*

THE ARMILLERY SPHERE

WHAT: An odd choice of sculpture for a Savannah square

WHERE: Troup Square, Savannah, GA

COST: Free

NOTEWORTHY: If the Armillary Sphere appears rather mystical or arcane, you won't be surprised to know that it features heavily in *Ineritas*, a series of young adult fantasy novels by author Rick Garman. The Armillary Sphere even appears on the cover of the first book, *The Beginning of Sorrows*.

Armillary Sphere supposedly was intended to be used as a sundial. It's unclear why an armillary was chosen as an appropriate monument to put in the middle of the square in the first place. Some speculate that when former Georgia Governor George McIntosh Troup—for whom the square is named—went out of favor for his pro-slavery, anti-Native American views, it was decided that a neutral, inoffensive monument should be erected instead of a statue of Troup.

79

HOLY TARGET PRACTICE

Who shot the swan in the belfry of the oldest church in Georgia?

Ebenezer is a ghost town in Effingham County that was founded by the Salzburgers, a small group of Lutheran Protestants who came to colonial Georgia after being exiled from Catholic Salzburg in Austria. Built on the banks of the Savannah River, the German-speaking Salzburgers were economically successful for a while with farming, a sawmill, a gristmill, and silk production. The town suffered damage during the American Revolutionary War, however, and never recovered, and by the time Ebenezer was abandoned in 1855, it covered only a quarter of a square mile.

The town of Ebenezer may be gone, but its place of worship, Jerusalem Lutheran Church, still remains and is remarkably still in use. Completed in 1769, the church is the oldest church building in Georgia and the oldest continuous Lutheran congregation in the United States, with services still held every Sunday. The walls are twenty-one inches thick (no wonder it's still standing), and some of the original window panes are still intact.

One of the more curious features of the church is the swan-shaped weathervane on the belfry. During the Revolution, the church was used by the occupying British as a hospital and stable. Some soldiers must have been

---

The building was constructed with red bricks made from the area's clay, and visitors can still see the fingerprints of the people who handpacked them.

Left, *Even as Ebenezer fell apart around it, the formidably constructed Jerusalem Lutheran Church remained unshakable and continues to welcome worshipers.* Right, *The bullet hole from a British musket is still visible on the swan weathervane.*

JERUSALEM LUTHERAN CHURCH

WHAT: The oldest church in Georgia

WHERE: 2966 Ebenezer Road, Rincon, GA 313326

COST: Free

PRO TIP: Church services are on Sunday at 11:00 a.m.

bored and took shots at the metal swan, leaving a bullet hole. The damaged vane was replaced, but when the church was used by General Sherman during the Civil War, his soldiers used the swan for target practice again, this time shooting it to bits. Members of the congregation were able to dig up the original weather vane and restore it to the top of the belfry. The bullet hole remains as a reminder of the church's history.

80

THE BARBER ARTIST

Where can you see a permanent collection of sculptures by a famed Savannah folk artist?

One of Savannah's greatest artists is relatively unknown outside of the city and folk art circles, but his legacy and work are preserved almost exclusively thanks to one institution. Founded in 1867 and named after the American inventor and editor of *Scientific American*, Alfred S. Beach, the Beach Institute was the first official school for African-Americans in Savannah. It closed as a school in 1919, but it continues to educate today as the Beach Institute African-American Cultural Center. The Beach Institute hosts award-winning exhibitions for art, history, and historic preservation, but their most important responsibility is safekeeping the art of Ulysses Davis.

Ulysses Davis (1914–1990) was a barber in Savannah for nearly fifty years. During his free time, he would whittle wood into beautifully expressive works of art, although he would have never considered himself an artist. People would come to his barbershop not just to get haircuts but also to see his pieces lining the shelves like works in an art gallery. Davis used lumber from shipyards to carve many of his pieces. He also incorporated objects (such as his wife's jewelry) into some of the sculptures and added textural details using his barber shears. Davis carved furniture pieces and reliefs

THE BEACH INSTITUTE

WHAT: The primary protectors of one of Savannah's most underappreciated artists

WHERE: 502 East Harris Street, Savannah, GA 31401

COST: $7 adults, $5 students/seniors/military

NOTEWORTHY: Outside of Savannah, a few Ulysses Davis pieces are in the Smithsonian American Art Museum.

Left, *Along with the Beach Institute of African American Culture, Civil Rights leader W.W. Law also established the King-Tisdell Foundation, Ralph Mark Gilbert Civil Rights Museum, and the Negro Heritage Trail Tour.* Right, *A recreation of Ulysses Davis' barber shop sets the scene for viewing his wonderful sculptures.*

but mostly created historical, biblical, and fantastical figures. He carved mahogany busts of every single president and even personally presented a bust of Jimmy Carter to Carter's family. In 1988, Davis received the Georgia Governor's Award in the Arts. He never sold his extraordinary work, so few people outside of Savannah ever saw any of it. He once said of his sculptures, "These things are very dear to me. They're a part of me. They're my treasure. If I sold these, I'd be really poor."

When Davis passed away, his hundreds of works of art were entrusted to the King-Tisdell Cottage Foundation and the Beach Institute, where they keep a permanent exhibit. Most of the 238 works are kept in storage and rotated out. Very few of his pieces are in museums outside of Savannah and only occasionally are they taken on traveling exhibitions, so the Beach Institute is the only place to fully experience this singular artist.

Davis's barbershop and home no longer exist, and an important part of Savannah's African-American art history has been lost with them.

81

THE ROAD TO MULBERRY GROVE

Where did Eli Whitney invent the cotton gin?

One of the most important historical sites in Georgia, one that would hold ramifications for the shaping of the country, ironically can't even be visited. Mulberry Grove was a plantation just upriver from downtown Savannah that sat on land that is now owned by the Georgia Ports Authority. Nothing remains of the plantation except for the foundation of some of the buildings, but nonetheless the spot holds incredible significance.

Mulberry Grove Plantation was owned by Nathanael Greene, a major general of the Continental Army in the American Revolutionary War, and a close friend of George Washington. After Green passed away from sunstroke, his wife, Catherine, hired a tutor named Eli Whitney to educate their five children. With her husband gone, Catherine was having trouble harvesting her cotton crop, so Whitney came up with a solution—the cotton gin. Whitney's revolutionary invention quickly separated seeds from cotton fibers much more efficiently than with manual cotton separation. As a result, cotton became the most profitable crop in the South, but with more productivity and profit came more slaves, with the numbers increasing from 700,000 in 1790 to 3.2 million in 1850. Whitney's cotton gin changed the economy of the South into one that was irrecoverably reliant on slavery.

George Washington visited Greene's widow at the plantation after her husband's death from sunstroke.

This historical marker on the side of the road is the only indicator that a lost historic site is nearby.

The patenting of the cotton gin in 1793 was one of the major catalysts for the Civil War, but the location of its inception is largely forgotten even by locals. The only physical indication that Mulberry Grove was ever there is a historical marker on Highway 21 in Port Wentworth situated two miles from the actual location of the plantation. People can visit the marker, but no one is allowed on the private property. Perhaps someday the State of Georgia and the Georgia Ports Authority will decide to develop and preserve the site of Mulberry Grove and allow public access to this important (and controversial) historical location.

MULBERRY GROVE PLANTATION

WHAT: The lost origin of the cotton gin

WHERE: Eastside GA 21 at Graveyard Road, Port Wentworth, GA

COST: Free

PRO TIP: Even if you were allowed on the property, the only thing left of the plantation is the foundation of the house.

82

RETRO RESTING

What is the "hippest" motel in Savannah?

So much of downtown Savannah's architecture is tied up in eighteenth and nineteenth century history that it's a bit of a shock when you see a roadside motel that wouldn't be out of place on the Vegas Strip. Built in 1964, the Thunderbird Inn is hard to miss with its retro, gaudily aglow neon sign. The vintage 1960s hotel is delightfully stuck in a bygone era of beehives and Beach Boys and offers a respite from Savannah's more Antebellum landmarks—sometimes you need "groovy" instead of "grandiose."

The Thunderbird recently renovated its forty-two rooms, and they retain their retro appeal without sacrificing modern amenities. The lobby has '60s hits playing to add aural atmosphere, the walls are covered in era-appropriate art by SCAD students, and the rooms feature colorful vintage furnishings. If it didn't already feel like time travel, Moon Pies and RC Cola are left in the room for incoming guests in lieu of pillow mints. Then in the morning, the inn offers free Krispy Kreme donuts with coffee. (Did people in the 1960s really eat this much sugar?)

The Thunderbird Inn also has a mascot. If you are looking for a companion to take around Savannah, George Monk the Sock Monkey is available at the front desk to show you around town. Guests can take George

THE THUNDERBIRD INN

WHAT: A hip motel in a city of squares

WHERE: 611 West Oglethorpe Avenue, Savannah, GA

COST: Rates vary.

PRO TIP: They are pet friendly and have a dog run onsite.

Top left, *Unlike Vegas, what happens in Savannah . . . everybody hears about.* Top right, *The restored motel was made more inviting with splashes of vibrant color.* Bottom, *George Monk is ready to be your guide around town.*

Monk with them as they explore the city and are then encouraged to post pictures of the sock monkey on his very own Facebook page.

Even if you don't stay at the Thunderbird Inn, it's still worth taking a look at this classic example of mid-twentieth-century Americana, as it stands in bright contrast to the older, Victorian-era locations downtown.

The inn is outfitted with solar panels to make it more environmentally friendly.

83

NUMBER OF THE BEAST

How many yellow fever victims are *actually* buried in Colonial Park Cemetery?

Established in 1750 and closed to burials in 1853, Colonial Park Cemetery has so many idiosyncrasies that it is almost the platonic ideal of a creepy graveyard. An estimated 12,000 people are buried in the cemetery, but there are only about 700 headstones. The dimensions of the cemetery used to be bigger, but when Abercon Street was built along its border, the unmoved graves were merely paved over. The cemetery has its share of ghost stories, but who needs them when the real history is already so fascinating?

For example, the cemetery is full of victims from the days of dueling which, in Savannah, reportedly began in 1740 and continued until 1877. In fact, the south end of the cemetery was apparently a favorite spot for duels. One marker onsite tells the tragic story of James Wilde and his death from dueling as a reminder of Savannah's propensity for men with "too much honor."

During the Civil War and Sherman's March to Sea, Union soldiers used the cemetery as a camp area. Although it isn't completely confirmed that they are responsible for it, it is believed that some of the more mischievous soldiers vandalized the graves by moving

Bodies in tombs would be left until they completely turned to dust at which time new bodies would be interred, so there is no telling how many souls were buried in them.

Left, *"Nearly 700" indeed.* Right, *Rows of markers line the back wall. Some believe that they were moved from their graves with malicious intent, but it is an old cemetery and falling, crumbling gravestones need to be put somewhere.*

headstones or altering them by carving misinformation on them, with one man having lived to 421, another to 544, and one man having been born 1,000 years before his father.

The most macabre bit of history involves a subtly tweaked fact on a historical marker about yellow fever. According to the marker, "nearly 700" victims of the 1820 yellow fever epidemic were buried in a mass grave, but historical records allegedly show that exactly 666 people are buried in the grave. The implication is that the numbers were fudged so that nobody would associate the epidemic with the work of the devil.

COLONIAL PARK CEMETERY

WHAT: One of the most storied cemeteries in the country

WHERE: 200 Abercorn Street, Savannah, GA 31401

COST: Your soul . . . er, free.

PRO TIP: Because of Colonial Park Cemetery, Savannah is called the "city built upon her dead."

84

NORTH AND SOUTH

Why is Laurel Grove bisected by a highway?

Bonaventure and Colonial Park Cemetery may get all the attention from locals and tourists, but the underappreciated Laurel Grove Cemetery has as much beauty and historical significance as its more popular counterparts.

Laurel Grove was built in 1850 on a portion of the former Springfield Plantation. The land was purchased by the city when Colonial Park and other cemeteries filled up to capacity. The distance of Laurel Grove from the city was part of a new trend of burying the dead away from the general population, as it was then believed that cemeteries emitted "miasmas" that made people sick. The lovely landscape of the cemetery was designed to also serve as a public park, with lots of shrubbery and shady trees to make for nice picnic spots. All of Laurel Grove's available plots were sold during the Victorian era, so it also has a large amount of Victorian architecture and statuary that sets it apart from other cemeteries.

It may not initially seem odd that Laurel Grove is split into two sections by Highway 204, but the division of the cemetery was actually already inherent in its planning. Laurel Grove North was the burial place of Savannah's white citizens, while Laurel Grove South was set aside for African-Americans. Important Savannah figures buried in the north section include Juliette Gordon Low, founder of the Girl Scouts; James Lord Pierpont, composer of "Jingle Bells"; and "The Waving Girl" Florence Martus.

Laurel Grove is named after the native laurel oak trees that once inhabited the area.

Top, *Laurel Grove North is arguably more beautiful than the more popular Bonaventure Cemetery thanks to its design as a public park.* Bottom, *Laurel Grove South is not as opulent as its neighbor, but it is equally rich in historical significance.*

LAUREL GROVE CEMETERY

WHAT: A burial ground segregated by road and design

WHERE: North: 802 West Anderson Street, Savannah, GA/South: 2101 Kollock Street, Savannah, GA

COST: Free

NOTEWORTHY: A Keeper's House, Porter's Lodge, Gazebo, and Public Holding Vault, all built in 1853, are still used by the Department of Cemeteries.

There is also an entire section dedicated to 1,500 Confederate soldiers and eight generals who died during the Civil War.

Laurel Grove South is one of the oldest and most significant African-American cemeteries in the Southeast. Originally a scant four acres were set aside for Savannah's African-American community, but over the years it has gradually expanded to ninety acres and is now about the same size as the northern section. Laurel Grove South is still in use today and is the final resting place of many of Savannah's important African-American citizens, such as Andrew Bryan, founder of the First African Baptist Church, and W.W. Law, a leading force in the Civil Rights Movement.

85

THE "COOLEST" PLACE IN TOWN

What was the first building in Savannah to have air-conditioning?

Savannah summers can be unbearably hot and humid. Tourists unaccustomed to the sweltering fug may ask themselves, "My God, what did people do before air-conditioning?" Well, the short answer: "They suffered." It wasn't until May 28, 1927, that citizens of Savannah finally got a taste of that sweet, chill, artificial breeze that we all take for granted these days.

The Lucas Theatre opened its doors the day after Christmas in 1921. The lavish theater was built by Savannah native Arthur Melville Lucas, Jr., who at the time was president of the American Theaters Corporation. During his career in films, Lucas was responsible for building forty movie theaters, but the Lucas Theatre was the only jewel that bore his name. The theater was already renowned for its extravagant architecture and interior design, but Lucas made an innovative addition to really bring in the crowds—air-conditioning!

Air-conditioning, or refrigerated air, as they called it then, was nearly unheard of at the time. Most homes

---

THE LUCAS THEATRE OF THE ARTS

WHAT: The "coolest" place for the hottest tickets in town

WHERE: 32 Abercorn Street, Savannah, GA

COST: Depends on the show

NOTEWORTHY: Now owned by SCAD, the Lucas Theatre shows classic movies and is a venue for live music and operas.

Left, *The Lucas is still a great spot to catch a Saturday matinee.* Right, *Restoration on the Lucas has made it not only the "coolest" theater in Savannah, but also the most beautiful.*

and businesses wouldn't have AC until the 1950s. In fact, the Lucas Theatre was the first building in Savannah to install it. According to their press release at the time, "It was a big and costly installation, with more than a carload of machinery, but we feel that the Lucas Theater must always be the last word in entertainment with comfort. Come in Tomorrow—The weather's fine."

Man-made weather wasn't enough to keep the theater going indefinitely. The Lucas closed in 1976 and was slated for demolition, but ultimately it was saved and decades later became one of the premier theaters in Savannah again.

The first films shown at the Lucas were *Hard Luck* starring Buster Keaton and *Camille* starring Alla Nazimova and Rudolph Valentino.

86

RARE READS

Where is the best place to purchase rare and first edition books?

There is almost no treasure greater than a good book—you're holding one right now—and a great bookstore can feel like a dragon's horde. The atmosphere of a bookstore is almost as important as its stock, and in the case of The Book Lady Bookstore, it excels in both.

The Book Lady Bookstore was founded in 1978 by local poet Anita Raskin. Through her work as a book scout and her gradual acquisition of a massive book collection, Raskin earned the nickname "The Book Lady" from locals. Raskin ran the bookstore until she passed away in 2002. Her employee, Joni Saxton-Giusti, took over the business and the mantle of Book Lady.

Every customer who enters The Book Lady marvels at how closely it fits with their ideal of a used book store. Everything looks old but not decrepit. The place is stuffed to the gills with books but in an organized manner—not dirty random stacks. Old chairs and couches invite visitors to stay awhile, and if they choose to, they can ask for a cup of coffee or tea while they read. All the books in stock are carefully curated by the proprietors, covering a wide range of subjects, such as art, architecture, "hard-to-find" history, foreign places, science and nature, African-American studies, classic and new fiction, and more.

The Book Lady has arguably the best poetry selection in town thanks to its work with the Savannah Poetry Review.

Left, *A glass case behind the desk protects the rarest and most unique volumes.* Above, *The Book Lady moved into its current, quaint location when Gallery Espresso coffee shop relocated around the corner.*

Their section of Savannah and Georgia history is particularly rich.

For collectors, they carry and can acquire rare books, first editions, fine bindings, and signed copies. Some notable books in their collection include a 1905 first edition of "Rip Van Winkle" by Washington Irving and a copy of *Memoirs of the War in the Southern Department of the United States* by Henry Lee signed by his son, Confederate General Robert E. Lee.

The Book Lady also plays host to the local literary scene with regular author reading events, signings, and a book club.

THE BOOK LADY BOOKSTORE

WHAT: The ideal dusty, old bookstore (without the dust)

WHERE: 6 East Liberty Street, Savannah, GA

COST: Free to browse; books range from $0.50 to $1,000+

PRO TIP: Watch that first step walking into the store. It's a doozy.

87 THE ANTIQUE MANSION

What is inside the Noble Hardee Mansion?

Viewed from the outside, the Noble Hardee Mansion on Monterey Square looks like just another (albeit exceptional) historical Savannah house. The only clue that it is anything more is the small sign for an antique store hanging over a side entrance. When you enter Alex Raskin Antiques, you might expect the store to occupy maybe a portion of the lower floor, so you will be shocked when you find out that all four floors of the house hold a stunning array antiques.

Built in 1869, the Noble Hardee Mansion is considered "the last unrestored grand mansion" in Savannah. That becomes apparent when wandering the beautifully derelict halls and rooms of the house, where expensive and exquisite antiques line every wall. The ceilings have plaster missing, paint peels from the walls, and creaky floors make you question how much longer they can support the thousands of pieces of furniture, chandeliers, paintings, clocks, lamps, and rugs that fill every room. For all the talk about ghosts in the city, this mansion looks like a legitimate haunted house.

The dilapidated mansion is the most antique thing about Alex Raskin's shop, but that is also its most charming

ALEX RASKIN ANTIQUES

WHAT: A dilapidated, yet stately antique store in an unrestored mansion

WHERE: 441 Bull Street, Savannah, GA

COST: Free, unless you break something

NOTEWORTHY: Alex Raskin's mother was the original "Book Lady," so you may want to visit her bookstore next.

Above, *With four floors and dozens of rooms, Alex Raskin Antiques is a maze of wondrous items that you could get lost in for hours.* Right, *A small side entrance belies the true size of the shop inside.*

feature. Raskin has said that he hasn't restored the home because he is saving that fun job for whoever buys it from him—the mansion happens to be the most expensive item for sale at his store. If the mansion were to be restored, Savannah would lose one of its most eccentric and treasured homes, broken windows and all.

The mansion once played host to President Chester A. Arthur.

CAPTAIN FLINT'S LAST STOP

What restaurant was an inspiration for *Treasure Island*?

Readers of Robert Louis Stevenson's *Treasure Island* may remember the fate of the wicked pirate Captain Flint. According to his first mate, Long John Silver, Flint died upstairs in an inn in Savannah shouting, "Darby M'Graw, fetch aft the rum . . ." Many believe that the inn in question was actually the Pirate's House and that Stevenson was inspired to use it as a location after visiting Savannah. To prove the point, several rare early edition pages of *Treasure Island* are hanging on the wall of the Treasure Room at the Pirate's House restaurant.

The Pirate's House sits on the site of the Trustees' Garden, an experimental garden set up by James Oglethorpe in 1733, four months after arriving in Savannah. The gardener's house, called the Herb House, was established on the spot. The garden was modeled after Chelsea Botanical Garden in London with the hope that they would be able to produce silk and wine. No luck with those, but they were successful in growing peaches and cotton. By 1754, there was no more need for the garden, so the Herb House was expanded into an inn,

THE PIRATE'S HOUSE

WHAT: A theme restaurant with a legitimate pirate past

WHERE: 20 East Broad Street, Savannah, GA

COST: See menu

NOTEWORTHY: The upstairs gift shop used to be a jazz club founded by local jazz legend Ben Tucker and pianist Emma Kelly. Pirates and jazz make a great combination.

Left, *Did a fictional pirate really die here?* Right, *The Pirate's House has many dining rooms, some of which retain their historical character.*

just as Savannah was evolving into a port town. The inn and tavern were popular with seamen (and supposedly pirates), thus inspiring many rumors and stories throughout the years.

In 1953, Savannah's popular visionary Herbert Smith Traub and his business partner, Jim Casey, leaned hard onto the inn's infamous past and turned it into the Pirate's House restaurant. They even insisted that it was haunted by the ghost of Captain Flint—never mind that he was a fictional character. The restaurant has been a Savannah institution ever since, and if the pirate costumes seem kitschy, the Pirate's House at least has an abundance of historical credibility to back it up.

The Herb House, built in 1734, originally housed the gardener for the Trustees' Garden and is considered the oldest standing building in Georgia.

Why is the Troup Square dog fountain so fancy?

If you happen to be walking your dog through Troup Square just as it's getting thirsty, you and your pup will get to experience one of the smaller, lesser-known monuments in the city. A diminuative but beautifully decorative bronze fountain offers hydration to parched pets.

The Myer Drinking Fountain was a gift donated to Savannah by Mayor Herman Myers in 1897. It was placed in Forsyth Park and meant for humans to drink from. The bronze sculpture was a 9'5" single pedestal with drinking basins and a faucet. On top of an acroter was a 3-foot-tall statue of a maiden feeding a dove sculpted by George Fisher and cast by J.W.Fisk. The statue depicts the girl creating a pouch with her tunic for holding seeds while she holds a seed in her mouth to feed a bird perched on her wrist.

The fountain was taken down for repairs in the early 1980s but seemingly disappeared. In 1983, a smaller version of the fountain, sans maiden, was set up in Troup Square. It's not clear if the truncated fountain is a replica or if portions of the original Myer Fountain were used. If they are actual portions of the original, what happened to

---

Each October 4, the Blessing of the Pets takes place at the fountain.

All water fountains, human or otherwise, should be this pretty.

MYERS DRINKING FOUNTAIN

WHAT: A repurposed gift to the city

WHERE: Troup Square, Savannah, GA

COST: Free

PRO TIP: The fountain is really only meant for pets, but if you must drink out of it . . .

the statue of the maiden? The faucets and basins on the original fountain were four feet above the ground but are now at ground level for dogs to drink out of, making the Myer Drinking Fountain a beautiful monument to man's best friend.

BIRTH OF THE GIRL SCOUTS

Where is the home of the Girl Scouts founder?

If you are new to Savannah, you may initially wonder why there are so many troops of Girl Scouts wandering the city. Well, it's because they were born here—not the girls themselves, but the Girl Scouts of America.

The Girl Scouts were founded by Juliette Gordon Low in 1912 after she got fired up by her involvement with the Girl Guides patrols just becoming popular in Europe. She wanted to create something similar in Savannah, so when she returned home she immediately called her cousin, Nina Pape, who was a local teacher, and said, "I've got something for the girls of Savannah, and all America, and all the world, and we're going to start it tonight." Since that moment, the Girl Scouts have grown into a global movement that inspires and empowers girls all over the world. Oh, and they sell amazing cookies.

When Girl Scouts make the pilgrimage to Savannah, they come to visit the birthplace of their inspiring founder. Juliette Gordon Low, or "Daisy," was born in the house in 1860 and founded the Scouts there, but the gorgeous Regency mansion holds more historical significance besides her story. Previous residents of

---

The Juliette Gordon Low Birthplace was designated Savannah's first National Historic Landmark in 1965.

Even if Juliette Gordon Low hadn't founded the Girl Scouts, the house is loaded with historical legacy, so it was fortunate that the organization was able to save it.

the house include Savannah mayor James Moore Wayne, who would later serve as a U.S. Congressman and a Supreme Court Justice. Daisy's grandfather, William Washington Gorgon I, who founded the Central of Georgia Railway, also lived there.

In 1953, to save the house from demolition, the Girl Scouts bought and restored it with funds raised from pageants, fashion shows, dinners, community fairs, and bake sales (that's a lot of cookies). The Juliette Gordon Low Birthplace now serves as a museum owned and operated by the Girl Scouts of America.

JULIETTE GORDON LOW BIRTHPLACE

WHAT: The headquarters of everyone's favorite cookie dealership

WHERE: 10 East Oglethorpe Avenue, Savannah, GA

COST: $13–$20

PRO TIP: Don't go there expecting cookies to be available year-round. Many have made that mistake.

SOURCES

1. **The Palms of Victory Drive**
   "Victory Drive Historic Corridor Study" Thempc.org; "Victory Drive Revitalization Envisioned" *Savannah Morning News*, Nov. 7, 2014

2. **The Uncanny Echo of Rousakis Plaza**
   "Rousakis Plaza Echo Square" Atlasobscura.com; "Story Behind the Story" WTOC, Nov. 1, 2006

3. **The Cow That Loved Fleas**
   "Savannah Georgia: Flea Market Mascot Big Cow" Roadsideamerica.com; "History and About Keller's Flea Market" ilovefleas.com

4. **The Whole World in Savannah**
   "The Globe" Keepsavannahstrange.com; "Savannah, Georgia: World Globe Storage Tank" roadsideamerica.com; "Off the Beaten Path: Savannah's Big Globe" WJCL, Nov. 6, 2014

5. **Tread Lightly**
   "Behind the 'Stone Stairs of Death' Facebook Page" WTOC, Nov. 5, 2015; Savannah Stone Stairs of Death Race, Roughrunnersr4r.com/savannah-stone-stairs-of-death-race/

6. **Bomb at the Beach**
   "The Saga of the Tybee Bomb" *Garden & Gun*, April/May 2018; "For 50 Years, Nuclear Bomb Lost in Watery Grave" NPR, Feb. 3, 2008; "Sixty years later, is Tybee bomb still lurking?" *Savannah Morning News*, Feb. 25, 2018

7. **The Runway Graves**
   "There are 2 graves on a Savannah-Hilton Head airport runway. How did that happen?" *The State*, Oct. 20, 2017; "The Incredible Story Behind the Two Gravestones Embedded in the Savannah Airport Runway" *Southern Living*, March 16, 2018; "Dotson Runway Graves" Atlasobscura.com

8. **A Church with History**
   "Second African Baptist Church" Gosouthsavannah.com; "Second African Baptist Church" *Savannah Morning News*, Feb. 12, 2007; "Historic Second African Baptist Church" Visit-historic-savannah.com

9. **Trestle of Tragedy**
   "June 28, 1959: Meldrim's saddest day" *Savannah Morning News*, June 27, 2009; "50 years later, effects of train disaster linger" *Effingham Herald*, June 29, 2009

10. **The Secret Garden**
    "Forsyth Park's Fragrant Garden" Gosouthsavannah.com; "Garden of Fragrance in Forsyth Park" Savannahga.gov

11. **Museum or Car Lot?**
    "Savannah Classic Cars and Museum opens for a cruise down memory lane" *Savannah Morning News*, Feb. 8, 2018; Savannahclassiccars.com

12. **The Old Oak Tree**
    "Candler Oak/Conservation Easement" Savannahtree.com/programs/candler-oak-conservation-easements/; "The story behind the Candler Oak Tree" Scaddistrict.com, Feb. 12, 2019

13. **Savannah's St. Bernadette**
    "Port Wentworth, Georgia: Our lady of Lourdes Grotto Replica" Roadsideamerica.com; "Our Lady of Lourdes" Franciscanmedia.com; "Port Wentworth: Driving Tour brochure" Visitportwentworth.com

14. **Sugar Refinery Explosion**
    "What Caused the Imperial Sugar Dust Explosion?" Hughsenv.com, Jan. 27, 2015; "10 Years Later: The Aftermath of Georgia Imperial Sugar Explosion That Killed 14" *Insurance Journal*, Feb. 12, 2018; "Legacy Park memorial dedicated to Imperial Sugar victims" *Savannah Morning News*, Feb. 7, 2009

15. **Lighting the Way**
    "Old harbour Light, Emmet Park" Gosouthsavannah.com; "Old Harbour Light" Savannahgavisitors.com

16. **The Man in Ellis Square**
    "Johnny Mercer Life Size Statue Unveiled in Ellis Square" *Savannah Tribune*, Nov. 25, 2009; "Johnny Mercer (1909–1976)" *New Georgia Encyclopedia*, Aug. 12. 2003

17. **King-Tisdell Cottage**
    "King-Tisdell Cottage" Gosouthsavannah.com; "King-Tisdell Cottage: Museum of Black History" Visit-historic-savannah.com

18. **Moon River Geechee**
"Pin Point Heritage Museum"
Gosouthsavannah.com; "Pin Point
Heritage Museum" Atlasobscura.com

19. **Broadway on Bull Street**
Savannahtheatre.com/history; *The
Savannah Press*, November 11, 1911,
Advertisement; "Cornerstone Speech"
Teachingamericanhistory.org

20. **Thelma and Louise**
"Thelma and Louise" Scpictureproject.
org; "Hardeevile, South Carolina: Pink and
Gray Elephants" Roadsideamerica.com;
Facebook.com/pg/PapaandjoesFireworks

21. **Endless Runner**
"Community activist memorialized"
Savannah Morning News, April 17, 2007;
"The Bonaventure Jogger" Atlasobscura.
com; "Julie Backus Smith–Obituary"
Legacy.com

22. **What's the Password?**
Americanprohibitionmuseum.com;
"America's Only Prohibition Museum
Opens in Savannah" Savannah.com

23. **The Googly Eye Bandits**
"'Who did this?!': Someone put googly
eyes on a historic Georgia statue. Police
want answers." *The Washington Post*, Oct.
14, 2018; *The Daily Show*, Oct. 16, 2018

24. **Planet of the Geeks**
"Life on Planet Fun" Scad.edu/blog/life-
planet-fun; "Planet Fun doubles up the
nostalgia with new location" *Savannah
Morning News*, June 19, 2014

25. **A Face on the Wall**
"Tomochichi Federal Building and U.S.
Courthouse, Savannah, Ga." Gsa.gov;
"Jeremiah O'Rourke" Digital Archive of
Newark Architecture, Dana.njit.edu

26. **Treasure Island?**
"Blackbeard Island" *New Georgia
Encyclopedia*, March 28, 2017;
"Blackbeard Island National Wildlife
Refuge" Gosouthsavannah.com;
"Blackbeard: History of the Dreaded
Pirate" "Queen Anne's Revenge Project,
qaronline.org

27. **Buddy Cop Cars**
"Restored vintage cop cars return to
downtown Savannah" *Savannah Morning
News*, May 19, 2010; "Antique police cars
back where they belong" WTOC, May 19,
2010; Savannahpd.org/history

28. **Junk Fish**
"With this Tybee artist, it's easy to play
'Go Fish'" *Savannah Morning News*, Jan
16, 2008; "Ralph Douglas Jones: Happy
Fish Folk Artist" *Make Magazine*, Aug. 21,
2014, Youtube.com

29. **The Earthworks Fort**
"Fort McAllister State Park, Richmond
Hill" Gastateparks.org

30. **Just a Casual Stroll**
"Charles Fraser, the alligator and the story"
Bloghiltonheadagent.com, March 22, 2011;
"Charles E. Fraser, 73, Dies: Developer
of Hilton Head" *The New York Times*,
Dec. 19, 2002; "Man Walks with Gator"
Roadsideamerica.com

31. **Spirits of the Trees**
The Tree Spirits of St. Simons Island"
Goldenisles.com/discover/golden-
isles/tree-spirits-of-st-simons-island/;
"Sculptor Releases Mysterious Spirits
Already in Tree" Mymodernmet.com,
March 15, 2013

32. **Can You Hear Me Now?**
"Jekyll Island and the Opening of the
Transcontinental Telephone Line"
Jekyllislandhistory.com; "A Long-Distance
Call for the Ages: How Jekyll Island made
telephone history" Jekyllisland.com

33. **Devils on Wheels**
Savannahderby.com/history; "Back
on track: Ready for season debut, the
Savannah Derby Devils grow, evolve over
decade" *Savannah Morning News*, March
5, 2016

34. **The Sloth of Skidaway**
"The Giant Sloth Mystery Brought Me
Back Home to Georgia" *Smithsonian*,
May 1, 2019; Skidaway Island State
Park, Facebook.com, Nov. 22,
2017; "Eremotherium eomigrans"
Floridamuseum.ufl.edu"

35. **Call of the Wild**
"Oatland Island: History and Relationship
to Savannah" Armastrongtourguide.
wordpress.com; "Oatland Island's Wild,
Wild Life" *Savannah Magazine*, Nov. 8,
2018; "Oatland Island wolf pups named"
WTOC, July 21, 2016

36. **Kehoe House Disco**
Kehoehouse.com/history; "Historic
William Kehoe House" Visit-historic-
savannah.com; "William Kehoe House"
Ghost.hauntedhouses.com/georgia_
savannah_kehoe_house#

37. The Girl Who Waved
"Savannah Georgia's Waving Girl on River Street" Tripsavvy.com; "The 'Waving Girl' Monument, Savannah" Gosouthsavannah.com; "Putting the Waving Girl on pedestal" *Savannah Morning News*, Aug. 7, 2014

38. Got Mail?
"Big mailbox on Quacco Road is a head-turner" *Savannah Morning News*, April 30, 2007; "Savannah's giant cow mailbox is a head turner. So what's the story behind it? Good question" WJCL, May, 14, 2019

39. Say a "Little" Prayer
"'Smallest Church in America' re-dedicated after rising from ashes" *The Brunswick News*, April 15, 2017; "Discover Christ Chapel Church in Darien, Georgia" N-georgia.com/christ-chapel-smallest-church.html; "Suspicious fire destroys Smallest Church in America" *Coastal Courier*, Nov. 30, 2015

40. The Bench
"Forrest Gump & Savannah" Gosouthsavannah.com; "Where is the real 'Forrest Gump' bench?" *Entertainment Weekly*, June 2, 1995

41. The Presidential Dive Bar
"Pinkie Master's: The Dive bar With A Presidential Past" *Imbibe Magazine*, July 11, 2016; "Jimmy Carter plaque back in Savannah's Pinkie Masters on St. Patrick's Day" *Savannah Morning News*, March 17, 2017; "Savannah's Pinkie Masters: The rest of the story" *Savannah Morning News*, Jan. 10, 2016; "Savannah bar recalls Jimmy Carter visit on St. Patrick's Day" *The Seattle Times*, March 17, 2017

42. An Outsider's Memorial
"Pay to Live: The Black Holocaust Memorial of Savannah, Georgia" Medium.com, Nov. 17, 2014; "SavArtScene: Work of Savannah's James 'Double Dutch' Kimble is an overlooked treasure" *Savannah Morning News*, Sept. 3, 2016

43. Savannah Underground
"The Mysterious Tunnels of Savannah" Ghostcitytours.com/savannah/haunted-places/haunted-tunnels/; "Beneath the Surface" *Savannah Magazine*, March 15, 2017; "Under Our Noses; Savannah's Tunnels" WTOC, July 26, 2011; "Old Candler Hospital" Blueorbtour.com/old-candler-hospital/

44. Gallery of Drunken Napkin Art
"Abe's on Lincoln" Atlasobscura.com/places/abes-on-lincoln; "Drinking, Drawing, and History; Napkin Art at Abe's on Lincoln" Medium.com

45. Chad's Magic Treehouse
"The Storybook Cottage" *Savannah Magazine*, March 15, 2017; Diamond in the Rough" *South Magazine*, March 14, 2018; "Diamond Oaks Treehouse Skylight Suite" Airbnb.com

46. The Haunted "Boo-ery"
Moonriverbrewing.com/aboit-us/the-ghosts/; "Moon River's Haunted History" Travelchannel.com/shows/ghost-adventures/articles/moon-rivers-haunted-history; "The Haunted Moon River Brewing Company" Ghostcitytours.com/savannah/haunted-places/haunted-restaurants/moon-river-brewing-company

47. The Castle in the Woods
"Powder Magazine" Abandonedsoutheast.com; "Tommy Barton column: City's tiny castle in the woods deserves to be seen" *Savannah Morning News*, May 19, 2018; "Savannah Powder Magazine, 1898" Vanishingcoastalgeorgia.com

48. Cinematic Treats
"Our History" leopoldsicecream.com; "Savannah Sweets: Ice cream and movie fans love Leopold's" *USA Today*, Sept. 18, 2014

49. Flying Fortress
Mightyeighth.org; "14 Things to Know About the national Museum of the Mighty Eighth Air Force" Visitsavannah.com; "Pooler's Mighty Eighth Museum celebrates 10 years with B-17" *Savannah Morning News*, Jan. 16, 2019

50. Reality Realty
"Savannah's Extreme Makeover house sold for $442,000" *Savannah Morning News*, Aug. 30, 2013; "'Extreme' Satisfaction" *Savannah Magazine*, March 6, 2017; "Extreme Makeover Home Edition Savannah Style Part 1" WJCL, Feb. 10, 2011, Youtube

51. The Heartbroken Girl
"Bonaventure Burial: Corrine Elliott Lawton" Savannah.com; "Grave of Corrine Elliott Lawton" Atlasobscura.com; "The Truth Concerning the Death of Corinne Elliott Lawton" Certainpointofview.com

52. The Atom Smashers
"Savannah, Georgia: 'Home of the Atom Smashers' Sculpture" Roadsideamerica. com; "History of SCJ" Internet.savannah. chatham.k12.ga.us/schools/jhs/Pages/ HistoryofSolCJohnsonHighScool.aspx; "31 Unbelievable High School Mascots" Mentalfloss.com

53. Tomochichi's Boulder
"Tomochichi's Monument" nscdaga. org/programs-projects/tomochichis-monument/; "Tomochichi: Death and Burial" Georgiahistory.com; "Tomochichi (ca. 1644–1739)" *New Georgia Encyclopedia*, Feb. 21, 2018, Georgiaencyclopedia.com

54. Oinks in Ossabaw
"Ossabaw Island Hog" Livestockconservancy.org; "Animals–Ossabaw Island Pigs" Ossabawisland.org/ island/ossabaw-pigs/; "Ossabaw Island" *New Georgia Encyclopedia*, July 17, 2003; "Projects" Ossabawisland.org/island/ projects/

55. From Ogeechee to Savannah
Socanalmuseum.com; "Savannah and Ogeeche Canal" Georgiatrails.com; "Savannah-Ogeeche Canal: Marker" Georgiahistory.com

56. The "Sears" House
"Sears Mishap House Myth" Atlasobscura.com; "Savannah, Georgia: House with Upside-Down Windows" Roadsideamerica.com; "The Whole Kit and Caboodle Susan Stamberg's House Came in a Kit, From the Beams to the Bolts. Maybe Yours Did Too" *The Washington Post*, Feb. 7, 2002

57. Walking "Bawk"wards
Flanneryoconnorhome.org/about; "Teaching a chicken to walk backwards" *National Catholic Reporter*, May 21, 2010; "Do You Reverse? (1932)" British Pathé, Youtube.com

58. Blood Suckers Museum
"U.S. National Tick Collection" Atlasobscura.com; "This Tick Collection in Georgia Contains Nearly Every Species Known to Science" Mentalfloss.com; "A museum of blood-sucking nightmares: the US National Tick Collection" CNN, Sept. 15, 2017; "Unites States National Tick Collection" Cosm.georgiasouthern.edu/ usntc/

59. Pitches at Pulaski
"America's Pastime at Fort Pulaski" Nps. gov; "Baseball and the American Civil War" American Battlefield Trust, Battlefields. org; "The National Pastime, Amid a National Crisis" *The New York Times*, May 9, 2014; "Civil War Baseball" National Museum of American History, Aug. 2, 2012

60. Shell Shock
"'World's Largest Boiled Peanut' to be unveiled at Bluffton Farmers Market on Aug. 22" *The Island Packet*, Aug. 20, 2013; "Bluffton's 'World's Largest Boiled Peanut' worse for wear after TV appearance" *The State*, July 16, 2014; "Creating the 'world's largest boiled peanut'" *Bluffton Today*, Aug. 21, 2013

61. Dashing Through the Snow?
"Local historians claim Savannah true home of 'Jingle Bells' song" *Atlanta Journal Constitution*, May 11, 2017; "Jingle Bells: A Thanksgiving Carol" Snopes.com; "James Lord Pierpont and the mystery of 'Jingle Bells'" Uuworld.org, Dec. 15, 2014

62. Haitian Heroes
"Haitian Monument, Savannah" Gosouthsavannah.com; "A Tribute to Haitian Soldiers for Heroism in the American Revolution" The44diaries. wordpress.com

63. Pump and Pet
Mosley's World Famous Animal Exit Farm, Facebook.com; "Mosley's petting zoo ranks in top places to visit" *Metter Advertiser*, April 29, 2015; "55 Secrets of the Georgia Coast" *Atlanta Magazine*, May 14, 2015

64. The Down-South Submarine
"Kazoo factory tunes into Beaufort County" *Bluffton Today*, Oct. 7, 2010; "Great Moments in Kazoo History" Mentalfloss.com

65. Cocktails and Poetry
"Bonaventure Cemetery–Cocktail Hour Graveside (w/Shannon Scott)" Bonaventure Cemetary Journeys, Youtube.com; "Must See Tombs in Savannah's Bonaventure Cemetery" Gallivanter.travel; "Conrad Aiken" Poets. org/poet/conrad-aiken; "Conrad Aiken: Marker" Georgiahistory.com

66. The Little Door to Nowhere
Personal communication with neighborhood shop owner

67. **A World Divided**
"'A World Apart' World War II Monument, Savannah" Gosouthsavannah.com; "A World Apart" Artandarchitecture-sf.com

68. **Graveyard of Trees**
"Driftwood Beach" Goldenisles.com/things-to-do/beaches/driftwood-beach/; "Driftwood Beach" Atlasobscura.com

69. **The Trident of Time**
"Visit the King Neptune Statue at Shelter Cove Harbour" Hiltonheadisland.com; "King Neptune Sundial" Atlasobscura.com

70. **Roots in Georgia**
Georgia State Parks & Historic Sites Division - Georgia DNR, Facebook.com, March 9, 2013; "6 Famous Film Locations in Georgia's Great Outdoors" Exploregeorgia.org

71. **Graveface**
"The Owner of Graveface Records Tells Us Why Savannah Is More Than Just a Sleepy Southern Town" *Fodor's Travel*, June 12, 2017; "Inside the Creepy Underground World of Serial Killer Art, Where Manson Means Money" *The Observer*, Oct. 29, 2018; "Graveface Records brings taxidermy, VHS tapes, oddities to Charleston" Postandcourier.com, July 3, 2018

72. **Where in the World?**
Vjduncan.com; "A World to the Wise" *The New York Times*, Oct. 13, 2002; "Jane Fishman: To John Duncan, history is life" *Savannah Morning News*, March 23, 2019

73. **The Seamen's Bethel**
Seamanshouse.org/our-history/; "Seaman's House a refuge for mariners" *Savannah Morning News*, March 1, 2014; Coalition Of Maritime Port Assistance & Seaport Services, Savannahcompass.org/international-seamans-house.html

74. **Choo Choo at the Roundhouse**
"Georgia State Railroad Museum!" Savannah.com; "Georgia State railroad Museum" Coastal Heritage Society, Chsgeorgia.org

75. **It's Maritime in Savannah**
Shipsofthesea.org; "Ships of the Sea Maritime Museum" Gosouthsavannah.com; "Ships of the Sea Museum" Visit-historic-savannah.com;

76. **Home of the Bananas**
Thesavannahbananas.com/grayson-stadium/; "Integration of Professional Baseball in Savannah, Georgia" Armstrongtourguide.wordpress.com, "borat baseball" Youtube.com

77. **Revolutionary Bar**
"Peter Tondee (ca. 1723-1775) *New Georgia Encyclopedia*, georgiaencyclopedia.com, Feb. 10, 2003; "Sons of Liberty Meet in Savannah" Todayingeorgiahistory.com

78. **Sphere in the Square**
"Troup Square" Savannah.for91days.com; "Troup Square" Savannah.com/troup-square/; "Armillary sphere" Britannica.com

79. **Target Practice at Church**
"Jerusalem Lutheran Church" visitebenezer.com; "Rincon, Georgia: Oldest GA Church – Shot Steeple Swan" Roadsideamerica.com; "Ebenezer" *New Georgia Encyclopedia*, March 18, 2005

80. **The Barber Artist**
Beachinstitute.org/exhibits; "Savannah's History: The Beach Institute" Savannah.com; "The Treasure of Ulysses Davis" Folkartmuseum.org; "SavArtScene: Savannah's Beach Institute offers rare exhibit of Ulysses Davis folk art collection" *Savannah Morning News*, March 3, 2018

81. **The Road to Mulberry Grove**
"Savannah's hidden history: Mulberry Grove" WSAV, Feb. 13, 2018; Mulberrygrove.org/about.html; "Mulberry Grove Plantation" Georgiahistory.com

82. **Retro Resting**
Thunderbirdinn.com/history; "Savannah, Georgia's Thunderbird Inn Might Be the Hippest Retro Hotel in America" Destination Strange, June 6, 2015, Maps.roadtrippers.com

83. **Number of the Beast**
"Historic Colonial Park Cemetery" Visit-historic-savannah.com; "Colonial Park Cemetery" Atlasobscura.com; "Colonial Park Cemetery" Gosouthsavannah.com; "Ghosts in the Graveyard: The Haunted History of Savannah's Colonial Park Cemetery" The Lineup, The-line-up.com/colonial-par-cemetery; "The Ghosts of Colonial Park Cemetery" Ghostcitytours.com

84. **North and South**
"Laurel Grove North Cemetery" Gosouthsavannah.com; "Laurel Grove South Cemetery" Gosouthsavannah.com;

"Laurel Grove North cemetery"
Savannahga.gov

85. **The "Coolest" Place in Town**
"Our History" Lucastheatre.com/history

86. **Rare Reads**
"Our Story" Thebookladybookstore.com;
"The Book Lady still strong after 40 years
of business" Scaddistrict.com, Oct. 9, 2018

87. **The Antique Mansion**
Alexraskinantiques.com; "Alex Raskin
Antiques" Atlasobscura.com; 'The Faded
Grandeur Of Noble Hardee Mansion"
Romantichomes.com; The Decaying
Mansion of Antiques: A Hidden Gem of the
Deep South" Messynessychic.com, June
26, 2014

88. **Captain Flint's Last Stop**
"The History of the Pirate's House"
Thepirateshouse.com/history/; "The
Pirate's House" Atlasobscura.com

89. **A Fountain Fit for Dogs**
"Myers Drinking Fountain"
Memorialdrinkingfountains.wordpress.
com, Sept. 28, 2014; "Troup Square"
Savannah.com/troup-square/;
Savannahga.gov/768/Monuments

90. **Birth of the Girl Scouts**
"Juliette Gordon Low" Girlscouts.
org; "About the Birthplace"
Juliettegordonlowbirthplace.org; "Juliette
Gordon Low Birthplace" Visit-historic-
savannah.com/juliette-gordon-low-
birthplace.html

INDEX

PUMP AND PET (page 148)